MARY

Personalities of the New Testament

D. Moody Smith, General Editor

Mary

Glimpses of the Mother of Jesus

Beverly Roberts Gaventa

Fortress Press   **Minneapolis**

MARY
Glimpses of the Mother of Jesus

First Fortress Press edition 1999

Cover design: Michael Mihelich

ISBN 0-8006-3166-8

The Library of Congress Cataloging-in-Publication data for the hardcover edition of this volume will be found at the end of the book.

The paper used in this publication meets the minimum requirements of American National Standard for Information Sciences—Permanence of Paper for Printed Library Materials, ANSI Z329.48-1984.

Manufactured in the United States of America   AF 1-3166

03   02   01   00   99   1   2   3   4   5   6   7   8   9   10

For Matthew

Contents

Preface

Qoheleth observed that "of making many books there is no end." His statement might well have been made solely for books about Mary, the mother of Jesus. Despite that fact, books on Mary by Protestant biblical scholars are exceedingly rare. Particularly for that reason, a few words about my own interests and perspectives may be appropriate.

I do write as a Protestant. In most areas of biblical scholarship that distinction no longer seems meaningful, but the differences between Protestant and Catholic perspectives on Mary remain significant. In the process of researching and writing this book, I have learned a great deal from Catholic traditions about Mary and Catholic discussions of Mary. Friends have talked with me about their own deep loyalties to Mary as well as their deep antipathy to the way in which Marian tradition has figured in the negative assessment and treatment of women. Colleagues have tolerated naive questions and explained features of Marian tradition that must to them be painfully obvious.

While I am profoundly grateful for all of that assistance, this necessarily remains the work of a Protestant and my questions are those of a Protestant. For example, readers will find almost no attention to the question of whether Mary continued to be a virgin after Jesus' birth. I respect such concerns, but they are not mine, and I will consistently point to discussions of them elsewhere. I hope those omissions will not seem dismissive of the traditions of others and that they will be balanced by what may be fresh questions and insights elsewhere. I also hope that my attention to this topic will generate interest among Protestants in an important and neglected figure.

I also write as a mother. My profound connection with my child makes it impossible for me to do otherwise, and I cannot pretend to distance myself from certain aspects of these texts. When Matthew's Gospel depicts the bloody Roman sword in Bethlehem and the threat to Jesus, a cold fear grabs me. When Luke describes Mary's puzzlement over the son who is both hers and not hers, I worry with her and for her. Some may find this lamentably sentimental. For me it is simply a fact of life.

Many times in the course of developing this book, I have been asked whether my approach is feminist. As often as the question arises, I stumble through it. The range of definitions of what is feminist is such that I scarcely know what to say. I understand myself to be a feminist in the sense that I am committed to the realization of the full equality of women and men in life together. Feminist analysis, however, very often has come to refer to work that is particularly concerned with exposing the androcentric and patriarchal values of biblical texts. While I do occasionally address such issues, they do not provide the driving force for this work.

I expect that readers will decide this question based on their own assumptions about what constitutes a feminist reading. On one occasion when I lectured on Mary, one member of the audience identified my approach as feminist and another, in response to the very same lecture, commented: "*That* certainly isn't feminist!" Probably much the same division of opinion will occur here.

I find myself in an awkward position. To be sure, I abhor the assumption in Matthew's Gospel that Joseph is free to dispose of Mary as he sees fit (although it turns out that the angel has something to say about that!). And I would delight in hearing the content of Mary's pondering. On the other hand, I am convinced that these stories contain much that instructs and edifies readers of every generation. My focus, then, has less in common with a feminist hermeneutics of suspicion than it does with what Daniel Boyarin has termed a "generous critique."[1]

In my work on this project, as in much of my study, I find my own experience reflected in the poignant story of Kathleen Norris. In her book *Dakota: A Spiritual Geography,* Norris describes returning to the church of her grandmother only to find herself extremely uncomfortable with the constant talk of a male savior. She could not bring herself to give up on the church, however, because the "strong old women" kept drawing her in. "Their wellworn Bibles said to me, 'there is more here than you know.' "[2] I hope readers will find that observation to be true of these glimpses of Mary: there is more here than you know.

To make this book accessible to readers outside as well as within the guild of biblical scholarship, I have used notes only to identify primary texts and scholarly treatments on which I draw directly, not to chronicle scholarly debates. The bibliography provides suggested readings in a variety of areas in order to make further reading easily available. As set forth on page iv above, all biblical quotations are taken from the New Revised Standard Version unless otherwise indicated.

It would never have occurred to me to write a book on Mary had not D. Moody Smith invited me to contribute to this series. I want to thank him for not-so-subtly nudging me into an undertaking that has proved fascinating, for his editorial oversight, and especially for his patience with seemingly endless delays.

C. Clifton Black and Patrick J. Willson read and responded with care and thoughtfulness to earlier drafts of the manuscript, and I am profoundly grateful for their generosity. I am also indebted to Charles B. Cousar, Martinus C. de Boer, Luke Timothy Johnson, Ross Shepard Kraemer, J. Louis Martyn, Kathleen E. McVey, and Daniel L. Migliore, all of whom read and commented on substantial portions of the manuscript. In addition, I wish to thank Raymond E. Brown, Rebecca S. Chopp, Shirley C. Guthrie, E. Elizabeth Johnson, Steven J. Kraftchick, Lucy Rose, Katharine Doob Sakenfeld, and George W. Stroup for conversations that helped to move the project along. Because the writing of this book has extended over several years, I fear I may have omitted names from these acknowledgments, for I have leaned heavily on the expertise of many. I especially want to thank the many students and others who probably have no idea how encouraging has been their interest in this project.

As I was in the final stages of completing the manuscript, word came of the sudden death of Charles Merritt Nielsen, my dear friend of nearly two decades. In this project, as in much else in my life, I was enriched by his wide-ranging knowledge and his utterly irrepressible and irresistible wit. Along with his family and a veritable host of friends, I shall miss him always.

Numerous organizations and institutions have indulged me as I tried out portions of this book in earlier versions. I was particularly pleased to be invited by John J. Collins to read a paper on Mary in Luke-Acts at the annual meeting of the Catholic Biblical Association in 1990. Portions of an earlier draft were given as the Oreon E. Scott Lectures at Texas Christian University in 1992, and I am particularly appreciative of the warm hospitality of Dean Leo Perdue and Professor William Baird, my hosts on that memorable occasion. I also benefited from invitations to lecture at the Interpreting the Faith Conference at Union Theological Seminary (Virginia), at the Shalom Center of Augustana College, at St. Mary's University's Ecumenical Center for Marian Studies (San Antonio), at Culver-Stockton College, and at Lancaster Theological Seminary. Members of the New Testament Colloquium at Princeton Theological Seminary read and critiqued the chapter on the Protevangelium of James in a constructive session. These have been genuinely congenial and instructive occasions, and I am pleased to have an opportunity to make public my gratitude.

I began work on this book during a sabbatical leave granted by Columbia Theological Seminary, and I am grateful to President Douglas W. Oldenburg and the trustees for that opportunity. During that leave, Gene M. Tucker and Carl R. Holladay of Emory University provided space in which to work uninterrupted, an act of uncommon hospitality. Following a change of institutional affiliation, the manuscript was completed on a sabbatical leave from Princeton Theological Seminary, and I want to thank President Thomas W. Gillespie and the trustees for making that leave possible. The libraries of Emory University, Columbia Theological Seminary, and Princeton Theological Seminary generously assisted in the location of a wide range of materials. In particular, I benefited from the skill of Katherine Skrebutenas of Speer Library at Princeton, the most welcoming and generous reference librarian of my acquaintance. Kim Olson, David Riggs, and David Freedholm provided able research assistance with a multitude of details; I am especially indebted to David Freedholm for his substantial work on the bibliography and to Michael Daise for his work on the indexes.

Daily I rely on the loving support of my husband, William Carter Gaventa, and our son, Matthew Roberts Gaventa. Although many people have helped me to see Mary more clearly, it is from Matthew that I have learned most of what I know about being a mother.

NOTES

1. Daniel Boyarin, *Carnal Israel: Reading Sex in Talmudic Culture* (Berkeley: University of California Press, 1993). Boyarin defines a "generous critique" as one "that seeks to criticize practice of the Other from the perspective of the desires and needs of here and now, without reifying that Other or placing myself in judgment over him or her in his or her there and then" (p. 21).
2. Kathleen Norris, *Dakota: A Spiritual Geography* (New York: Ticknor and Fields, 1993) 94.

Abbreviations

AB	Anchor Bible
ANF	*Ante-Nicene Fathers*, ed. Alexander Roberts and James Donaldson
BAGD	W. Bauer, W. F. Arndt, F. W. Gingrich, F. Danker, *Greek-English Lexicon of the New Testament*
BNZW	Beihefte zur *Zeitschrift für die neutestamentliche Wissenschaft*
BTB	*Biblical Theology Bulletin*
BZ	*Biblische Zeitschrift*
CBQ	*Catholic Biblical Quarterly*
EKKNT	Evangelischkatholischer Kommentar zum Neuen Testament
ExpTim	*Expository Times*
ICC	International Critical Commentary
IRT	Issues in Religion and Theology
JAAR	*Journal of the American Academy of Religion*
JB	Jerusalem Bible
JBL	*Journal of Biblical Literature*
JES	*Journal of Ecumenical Studies*
JR	*Journal of Religion*
JRS	*Journal of Roman Studies*
JSNT	*Journal for the Study of the New Testament*
LCL	Loeb Classical Library
LXX	Septuagint

NAB	New American Bible
NCB	New Century Bible
NEB	New English Bible
NIGTC	New International Greek New Testament
NIV	New International Version
NJB	New Jerusalem Bible
NKJV	New King James Version
NovT	*Novum Testamentum*
NRSV	New Revised Standard Version
NTS	*New Testament Studies*
PG	*Patrologia Graeca*, ed. J. Migne
REB	Revised English Bible
RSV	Revised Standard Version
SBLDS	Society of Biblical Literature Dissertation Series
SBLSPS	Society of Biblical Literature Seminar Papers Series
SNTSMS	Society for New Testament Studies Monograph Series
TEV	Today's English Version
TS	*Theological Studies*
WBC	Word Biblical Commentary

Abbreviations for biblical and other early Jewish and Christian texts may be found in "Instructions for Contributors," *AAR/SBL Membership Directory and Handbook* (1994) 227–30.

Mary
Glimpses of the Mother of Jesus

CHAPTER 1

The Quest for Mary

In paintings and poetry, with song and sculpture, from rarified theological ruminations to the most vulgar piety, women and men have pondered the mystery of Mary, the mother of Jesus of Nazareth. Twenty centuries of Christian history have witnessed an astonishing variety of expressions to the church's fascination with this woman.

As early as the second century, the writer of the Odes of Solomon, a collection of Christian hymns, described Mary as "a mother of great mercies" and declared her praise:

> She loved with salvation,
> and guarded with kindness,
> and declared with greatness.[1]

And as recently as the 1980s, the American poet Lucille Clifton composed a cycle of poems on the life of Mary, focusing less on the glory of Mary and her child than on the emotional turmoil of a woman whose life has been ripped out of her control.[2]

Artists' renderings of Mary have similarly reflected an immense range in interpretations. Early Christian art borrowed heavily from Greco-Roman portraiture to render Mary as Queen of Heaven. By contrast, for his pietà in St. Peter's, Michelangelo shunned such ethereal realms and presented her as a vulnerable, grieving mother. Henry Ossawa Tanner, an African-American painter working at the turn of the twentieth century, saw Mary as a terrified girl retreating into the corner of a peasant cottage as she is confronted by an apparition of pure light and an annunciation that overturns her life. Mary graces with her beauty the most prestigious museums of the world as well as the candles and T-shirts of ubiquitous tourist traps.

For a vast number of Christians, Mary occupies a central place in devotional life. However her reported appearances across the globe are to be explained, at the very least those events reflect the enormity of Mary's impact. Willa Cather's Sada, a Mexican woman living the life of a slave, explains to her archbishop, "Ah, Padre, every night I say my Rosary to my Holy Mother, no matter where I sleep!"[3]

Books and articles investigating Mary's life, her theological significance, her place in Christian devotion, and her psychological and social and historical importance come forth at a bewildering pace. A single figure measures the story: the holdings of the Marian library at the University of Dayton exceed 85,000 books and pamphlets.

In view of this superabundance of books written about Mary, the offering of yet another requires more than a word of explanation. What I undertake in this volume is a study of the treatment of Mary in four narratives of early Christianity: the Gospel of Matthew, the two-volume work consisting of the Gospel of Luke and the Acts of the Apostles, the Gospel of John, and the Protevangelium of James. I am concerned with the way each of these four narratives characterizes her, what role (or roles) she plays in the larger story, how she participates in the overarching movement of the story. That is to say, what distinguishes my project is that the method adopted here is more literary than either historical or theological. Although other books on Mary certainly contain insights of a literary nature, I am not aware of others that consistently work from a literary approach.

With the exception of the Protevangelium of James, in which Mary is the central character, each of these early Christian narratives permits us only a mere glimpse of Mary. I resist the temptation to exaggerate her importance, a temptation that is especially vigorous given the need to know more about women in early Christianity. I also resist neglecting her, as has been the tendency in much scholarly exegesis, particularly in Protestant circles where indifference greets most discussion of Mary.

The plural "glimpses" in my title is both intentional and essential. Each document offers a distinct portrait of Mary. John's Mary is no more interchangeable with Luke's than a painting of the Virgin of Guadalupe is interchangeable with an icon of the Queen of Heaven. In the chapters that follow, we shall see that Matthew portrays Mary entirely as the mother of Jesus whose maternity poses a threat to the status quo and who is threatened by that status quo in return. Luke assigns to Mary three distinct roles, those of disciple, prophet, and mother, but it is in her role as mother that the Lukan Mary enlivens the story by pondering events and questioning her son. At the wedding in Cana and at the cross, the Johannine Mary serves to heighten the awareness that Jesus is a real human being. The Protevangelium's Mary seems scarcely a real human being, so utterly set apart is she by her sacred purity.

Without diminishing in any way the distinctiveness of these glimpses, I also show that each of them is colored by the dynamic of scandal that runs so powerfully through early Christian writings. For Matthew, the scandal that surrounds Jesus' conception continues the history of apparent scandals that punctuate the long story of God's dealings with Israel. In Luke-Acts, the scandal that threatens Mary has to do with whether she will remain a disciple in spite of Jesus' scandalous behavior. Mary, the mother of a thoroughly human Jesus, is subsumed in the Gospel of John within the theological scandal inherent in the fact that the Word itself has become flesh. Much of the Protevangelium responds to the scandal that surrounds the pregnancy of a young woman dedicated to the temple itself. Here the tenor changes: while the canonical writers align themselves positively with these scandals, recognizing that they are scandals at the heart of faith itself, the author of the Protevangelium, by contrast, labors to dissociate Mary from even the slightest taint of a charge against her purity.

Each of the chapters that follow is concerned with one of these four narratives. Before turning to them, however, I want to distinguish the literary approach adopted here from the established tradition of "quests" for Mary, most of which have been historical or theological.

THE HISTORICAL QUEST FOR MARY

What historical information do we possess about Mary, the mother of Jesus? As a brief survey of the New Testament references to her will attest, the answer is that we know extremely little.

The earliest reference to Jesus' mother in any literature, and the only one in the Pauline letters, appears in Galatians, which was written sometime in the early 50s. In Gal 4:4 Paul comments that God's son was "born of a woman, born under the law." For the purposes of historical investigation, these phrases tell us only that Paul understands Jesus to have been born to a Jewish woman (see also Rom 1:3 and 9:5). The fact that he does not mention Mary's name does not necessarily mean that he does not know it, but neither can it be assumed that he knows it and declines to use it. Such details are no part of the point he is developing.

Chronologically, the next references to Mary appear in the Gospel of Mark, probably written in the late 60s or early 70s.[4] Mark includes two brief vignettes involving Mary. In Mark 3, the family of Jesus attempts to restrain him, believing him to be mad. Then Mary and Jesus' brothers stand outside the place in which Jesus is teaching, prompting Jesus' seemingly harsh comment that "whoever does the will of God is my brother and sister and mother" (3:35). When Jesus returns to Nazareth in Mark 6, the locals ask in astonishment, "Is not this the carpenter, the son of Mary and brother of James and Joses and Judas and Simon, and are not his sisters here with us?" (6:3).

To learn more about the historical Mary, we turn to the familiar narratives in the Gospels of Matthew and Luke and to John's Gospel for the story of the wedding at Cana and Mary's presence at the crucifixion of Jesus. Since each of these Gospels will be the subject of a closer reading in the chapters that follow, it is sufficient here to note that they offer little information for a historical reconstruction of the life of the mother of Jesus.

In Revelation the seer describes a vision of a woman "clothed with the sun, with the moon under her feet, and on her head a crown of twelve stars" (12:1). The woman gives birth to a son who is clearly a messianic figure, and then she flees to the wilderness under God's protection. To the extent that the child represents Jesus, the woman may be understood as Mary. Given the highly symbolic nature of this vision, however, even that assertion remains tentative. Certainly, whatever we make of the woman in Revelation 12, the passage contains no historical information about Mary.

Even if we take all of the available scraps of evidence as historically reliable, what emerges is slender indeed: the mother of Jesus was named Mary. At the time of Jesus' conception, she was a resident of Nazareth in the region of Galilee (Luke 1:26), although Matthew suggests Bethlehem as her home (see 2:1). She was engaged to and eventually married Joseph, and later she gave birth to other children (unless the brothers and sisters of Jesus are to be regarded as children of Joseph from a previous marriage or even perhaps as cousins).[5] We are given the names of no other relatives except that of Elizabeth, the mother of John the Baptist, who was her cousin. Mary's sacrifice of turtledoves or pigeons following Jesus' birth (Luke 2:24) suggests that she was from a poor family, as the sacrifice of a sheep was prescribed for those who could afford such (Lev 12:8). That sacrifice, as well as the comment that she and Joseph annually celebrated Passover in Jerusalem, suggests that she was devout. Ascertaining anything of Mary's attitude toward Jesus is virtually impossible. The stories in which Jesus declares that his family consists of those who do God's will (e.g., Mark 3:31–35) might be said to show her distance from his ministry, although her presence at the cross (John 19:25–27) and with the apostles in Jerusalem following the crucifixion (Acts 1:14) suggests that, at least eventually, she was counted among Jesus' followers.

As slender as even this historical reconstruction is, serious questions must be raised about a number of items within it. For example, the poor and marginalized occupy a major place in Luke's Gospel, which might mean that he deliberately identifies Mary with the poor. Similarly, the Jerusalem temple plays an important role throughout Luke's writings, which could mean that Luke exaggerates Mary's piety in order to highlight the temple. In other words, even the evidence we do possess cannot be treated at face value as unbiased historical reportage, because it is already laden with theological freight.

Women in Early Judaism

Can this meager evidence regarding the historical figure of Mary be enhanced by our knowledge of the social and religious situation of women in the various forms of Judaism in existence in the first century? A greater awareness of the living conditions of women in general would not provide us with additional details regarding Mary in particular, but it might help create a sense of understanding her larger environment. What possibilities lay before a young woman in her circumstances? What constraints limited her choices and prevented her autonomy? What valuation did her peers place on such a life as hers?

This line of inquiry has great potential, but it is fraught with even greater difficulties. First, we need to be aware of several problems with our interpretation of the evidence. Often we read anachronistically, employing contemporary Western values to assess people for whom these values would be utterly foreign. In addition, assessments of Jewish (or any other) evidence as reflecting "negative" and "positive" valuations of women overlook the fact that cultural assessments are seldom so simple. If some early Jewish writings appear to treat women as the property of their fathers and husbands, viewing them solely in economic terms, what should be said of the contemporary Western evaluation of women in the workplace? Is that not also a kind of reductionism by which women (like men) are of value only to the extent that they are economically productive?

Second, there is the temptation, especially for Christian scholars, to exaggerate the negative portrait of women in various forms of Judaism. Particularly since World War II, Christian scholars have become aware of their tendency to purchase a positive assessment of Christianity by means of denigrating Judaism, often in vicious terms. In the case of reconstructing the history of women, Christian scholars have often made Jesus and early Christianity look more "liberating" by contrast with what are depicted as "oppressive" and "patriarchal" forms of Judaism.[6]

Third, quite apart from the problems created by the perspectives interpreters bring to bear on these questions, the sources for reconstructing the history of Jewish women in this period present us with a variety of problems. As with any evidence regarding Jewish practices in the first century, the tendency has been to draw heavily on rabbinic writings that derive from a much later period. For example, the Mishnah, a collection of Jewish legal tradition, is first committed to written form about 200–250 C.E. The Babylonian Talmud comes into being several centuries later still, not before 500 C.E. While those later writings do contain information drawn from earlier periods, separating information that is historically reliable from that which is unreliable is virtually impossible.

Even if we could sift through the rabbinic writings and establish which were the earliest layers of tradition, we would still have the formidable task of distinguishing between *what the rabbis say* ought to be the case and what was the *actual practice* of Jewish women and men. For example, the Mishnah instructs that a girl who "has grown two hairs [i.e., in puberty] . . . is subject to all the commands prescribed in the Law" (Niddah 6.11),[7] but nothing enables us to know whether such instructions were actually followed or by whom. In the same manner, we have no way of knowing to what extent Jews observed the multitude of decrees regarding marriage, divorce, ritual impurity, contracts, and vows (*if* those decrees were already in existence in the first century). As Ross Shepard Kraemer has aptly put it, "rabbinic sources may at best refract the social realities of a handful of Jewish communities, and at worst may reflect only the utopian visions of a relative handful of Jewish men."[8]

In fact, recent findings, taken together with these methodological considerations, seriously undermine many generalizations often made about women in early Judaism. It is asserted, for example, that women would have been confined largely to the sphere of home and family. Evidence for this claim comes from Philo, who complains about an incident in which Jewish homes in Alexandria were searched, because the soldiers violated the custom that Jewish women lived "in seclusion, never even approaching the outer doors, and their maidens [lived] confined to the inner chambers, who for modesty's sake avoided the sight of men, even of their closest relations" (*Flaccus* 89; see also *On the Special Laws* 3.169–77).[9]

Philo writes from the context of Alexandria, however, and his comments about the practices of upper-class Jews in that city do not necessarily reflect practices elsewhere. On the contrary, papyrological evidence from Egypt and Asia Minor shows the involvement of women in commerce.[10] In addition, the Gospel narratives assume that women appear in public; Mary travels (apparently alone) to visit Elizabeth (Luke 1:39), Anna remains in the temple "night and day" (Luke 2:37), women accompany Jesus and support his ministry (Luke 8:2–3). One need not accept the historicity of these individual vignettes to recognize their assumption that it was credible to depict women in public places.

Comments about marriage practice need to be subjected to similar scrutiny. The Mishnah depicts a situation in which, when a young woman married, she passed from the governance of her father to that of her husband: "The father has control over his daughter as touching her betrothal whether it is effected by money, by writ, or by intercourse. . . . When she is married the husband exceeds the father in that he has the use of her property during her lifetime; and he is liable for her maintenance and for her ransom and for her burial" (Ketuboth 4.4).[11] Although her husband could divorce her, she could not divorce him. Her authority even over the possessions inherited by her or granted her as part of the marriage process would have been limited.

Again, however, evidence outside the Mishnah calls into question any assumption that these principles were uniformly maintained. An Egyptian papyrus from the first century B.C.E. records a divorce agreement in which the husband and wife mutually declare their consent to the terms of the divorce.[12] A recently published set of documents belonging to Babatha, a Jewish woman of the early second century, reveals a woman who controlled considerable wealth and who freely entered into litigation on behalf of herself and her son.[13] In other words, at least some women acted far more independently than the Mishnah would allow us to suppose.

Generalizations about the participation of Jewish women in religious life are also problematic. The Mishnah frames a general principle in terms of non-obligation: "All the obligations of a father towards his son enjoined in the Law are incumbent on men but not on women. . . ." (Qiddušin 1.7).[14] The Babylonian Talmud takes matters further by explicitly stating that parents are not obliged to teach their daughters, "Because it is written 'And ye shall teach them your sons' but not your daughters" (Qiddušin 29b).[15] To state that women are not obligated in effect serves to exclude them from full participation in the religious life of the community.

Here again we encounter the convoluted question of how to understand the evidence of rabbinic writings. Daniel Boyarin's recent study of sexual issues in talmudic culture elegantly recalls the way in which rabbinic writings depend on the interplay among conflicting judgments, actually canonizing dissent. To read isolated talmudic statements, then, is often highly misleading. Indeed, it is precisely in the context in which some rabbis would deny the study of Torah to women that Boyarin detects other, admittedly minority, voices.[16]

Evidence outside rabbinic literature further undermines the rabbis' portrait of women's absence from religious life. In a remarkable study of women in early Jewish synagogues, Bernadette J. Brooten adduces inscriptional evidence that women held offices in local synagogues in their own right and that the leadership of women was both religious and financial.[17] Equally surprising is the absence of evidence for the assumption that women and men were segregated in synagogue worship.[18] Did men and women worship together? We cannot be certain, but to assume they did not exceeds the evidence of extant sources.

Even this brief introduction to the retrieval and reconstruction of the history of Jewish women in the Greco-Roman world reveals that much important work is underway. Although the lives of Jewish women (indeed, of both women and men in the ancient Mediterranean world) in this period would have been circumscribed to an extent that most contemporary Westerners would find incomprehensible, it is far from clear that Mary's life must have been as restricted as scholars have sometimes assumed.

Recent Historical Investigations

As the preceding survey demonstrates, the New Testament makes only infrequent reference to Mary, and assessing that evidence within its historical and cultural setting is highly complicated. In their quest to understand as much as possible about Mary, biblical scholars have employed a variety of methods to analyze and assess such evidence as is available. Four recent examples will illustrate the range of these approaches and their conclusions.

1. *Mary in the New Testament*. In 1978 a panel of Roman Catholic and Protestant biblical scholars associated with the Lutheran-Roman Catholic dialogue in the United States published the results of their collaborative investigations under the title *Mary in the New Testament*.[19] The approach to the study of Mary in this volume is predominantly historical. That is not to say that the study is objective (as if such an approach were possible), but that the concern is with establishing what can be known about the life of Mary and especially about the history of traditions regarding Mary.

Mary in the New Testament works with an understanding of the Gospels pioneered in the earlier part of this century by form and redaction critics interested in the ways gospel traditions grew and were later shaped by the evangelists. The panel identifies three stages in this development: stage 1 consists of the actual events in the lives of Jesus and those around him; stage 2 is the period in which traditions were shaped and circulated prior to the writing of the Gospels; and stage 3 is that of the composition of the Gospels. The Gospels of stage 3 do, of course, contain information that derives from stages 1 and 2, and one concern of *Mary in the New Testament* is to distinguish among those stages wherever possible.

An example will help to clarify the procedure. In Acts 1:14 Luke includes Mary among those gathered in Jerusalem for the celebration of Pentecost. In *Mary in the New Testament* this reference to Mary is regarded as having a high degree of historical probability. Luke clearly does not have an interest in glorifying the place of Mary in the developing church, since this is the only time she appears in Acts. Because the reference serves no distinctive Lukan purpose, it may well come from early tradition (stage 1).[20]

Since the only access we have to stage 1 is by means of the Gospels, and since the evangelists and Christians prior to them almost certainly tailored materials to suit the needs of their communities, the probability of arriving at a reliable portrait of Mary is slender indeed. What can be seen, according to the panel, is a diversity of views of Mary in stage 3 with an increasing stress on Mary as a disciple of Jesus.

2. *The Illegitimacy of Jesus.* Jane Schaberg's work on the infancy narratives employs methods identical to those of the panel that produced *Mary in the New Testament,* but with startlingly different results.[21] In part these differences are due to the inevitable scholarly disagreements about which statements in the Gospels may be regarded as early (and therefore probably historically accurate) and which must be regarded as late (and therefore less likely to be historically accurate). This particular instance of scholarly disagreement also reflects the fact that Schaberg writes from an explicitly and self-consciously feminist stance.

Schaberg argues that Jesus was illegitimately conceived, most probably as a result of rape, during the period when Mary was engaged to be married to Joseph. This memory was preserved by the family of Jesus. In this pre-gospel stage (stage 2), Christians understood this conception to be entirely natural, but they also attributed it to the work of the Holy Spirit in cooperation with God's own plan. When Matthew and Luke wrote their Gospels, working independently of one another, they intended to pass along this tradition. Their own androcentric perspectives and diplomatic narrations, however, nearly cover over the tradition, so that Christians of later generations could freely develop the tradition of the virginal conception. The result is that, in Schaberg's view, the real story of Mary has been obscured.

3. *The Liberation of Christmas.* Schaberg shares with the interdenominational panel that produced *Mary in the New Testament* the goal of reconstructing the traditions that stand behind the Gospel narratives and discerning the intentions of the evangelists in their own use of those traditions. In his book *The Liberation of Christmas,*[22] Richard Horsley also employs a historical method, but here the goal changes. Rather than reconstructing the history of traditions behind the Gospel narratives, Horsley wants to identify the general socio-political settings that give rise to and are addressed by the infancy narratives. For example, in connection with the Matthean story of Herod's attempt to destroy the infant Jesus, Horsley provides a lengthy discussion of the oppressive nature of Herod's reign. Within that setting, he explores the way in which Matthew 2 posits a conflict between the messiahship of Jesus and the kingship of Herod. The questions here are historical,

then, not in the sense of reconstructing the history of Jesus' life but in the sense of understanding the "particular historical circumstances and social relations that provide the background from which the narratives emerged and to which they refer."[23]

Horsley's concern is with the infancy narratives as a whole rather than with their treatment of Mary, but his conclusions nevertheless have implications for an understanding of Mary. He rejects the characterization of the Lukan Mary as an ideal believer, which he finds "belittling," in favor of understanding "the world-historical significance of the events of deliverance in which Mary" and others are central figures.[24] Mary's action in giving birth to Jesus, the new Davidic ruler, places her over against the established system of power.

4. "Mother and Son." A final illustration of the historical quest for Mary comes from the work of Bruce Malina. In a series of books and articles over the last two decades, Malina has brought the insights of cultural anthropology to bear on reading the New Testament. His article "Mother and Son" uses this same approach to interpret the New Testament's comments about Mary.[25] Scholars who read the New Testament through the lenses of cultural anthropology are often distinguished from "historical critics," because the term *historical* is being used to refer somewhat narrowly to those who are reconstructing the history that is represented by the text or the history of the text. Malina's work does belong under the general rubric of historical approaches, however, because he shares the concern for historical events, even if his avenue to those events is distinctive.

Malina begins with the assumption that insights from contemporary anthropological study of the Mediterranean may be used directly to understand life in the Mediterranean in the first century: "if some feature exists in Mediterranean society and everything indicates that it always has been that way in the Mediterranean, it must have been [that way also] in the past."[26] Among the central features of Mediterranean society is its stress on kinship ties and gender-based roles; the focal institution is the family, and virtually all aspects of life are understood in terms of gender.

Malina uses these insights to account for much in the way Mary is presented in Luke in particular. God communicates with Mary only regarding procreation (Luke 1:28–37), and Mary complies with the wishes of God as women are intended to comply with the wishes of men (Luke 1:38). Like all women in her culture, she becomes an adult only when she also becomes a mother; hence, Elizabeth's greeting to her addresses her in terms of her impending motherhood (Luke 1:42). Because boys live within the realm of mother until they move into the male world, it is Mary rather than Joseph who confronts Jesus when he is found to have stayed behind in Jerusalem rather than returning home with his family (Luke 2:41–51). Every line that describes Mary does so exclusively in terms of stereotypical Mediterranean motherhood.

These four examples should give both a sense of the limits of our knowledge about the historical Mary and the range of the historical quest for Mary. Because in the chapters that follow I seek to answer questions that are quite different from those of the historical quest, I shall not offer a detailed response to each approach. I will note that I read some of these historical approaches with considerable skepticism. The ease with which Malina applies anthropological research on contemporary Mediterranean culture directly to first-century texts strikes me as especially problematic. Horsley's insistence that biblical scholarship has neglected the socio-political context in which Christianity emerged is important, but he sometimes seems to reduce the texts to stories of political conflict. My own focus on the narratives as they stand makes me less confident than the writers of *Mary in the New Testament* about our ability to separate early tradition from the additions of the Gospel writers; I am even more skeptical about Schaberg's thesis because it consists largely of an argument from silence.

These remarks should not be understood as a claim that historical and literary approaches are antithetical to one another. Although some scholars would posit just such a bifurcation, I do not. In fact, it will become clear that my own work has benefited from the analyses of several of these contributions.

THE THEOLOGICAL QUEST FOR MARY

The historical quest for Mary searches "behind" the biblical texts, seeking wisps of information about the historical Mary, about the way traditions emerged concerning her and how those traditions were later employed by the evangelists. The theological quest, by contrast, begins on "this side" of biblical texts in an attempt to assess Mary's place in Christian faith. The diversity within the theological quest is enormous: for some strands in Christian theology, the near-silence of the New Testament regarding Mary necessitates a comparable silence on the part of theologians; for others, the glimpses of Mary afforded by the New Testament provide only the starting point for intensive and extensive Marian reflection.

This section will sketch in a very general way some of the major issues in the theological quest for Mary. Because treatments of Mary differ significantly among the three major branches of the Christian church (Roman Catholic, Orthodox, and Protestant), my introduction to the theological quest will be organized along those three lines. Given the diversity of views within each of these branches (not to mention the history of their polemical discussions of Mary), this introduction will necessarily work with very large brush strokes that cover a mass of variations. The goal here is not a comprehensive discussion of the theological quest for Mary but an introduction that may clarify the distinctiveness of my own approach as well as illumine some points of inter-Christian dialogue and dispute.

As in discussing the historical quest, I make no attempt here to engage in critical dialogue with the theological quests for Mary. As a Protestant spectator of the discussions carried on largely in Roman Catholic and Orthodox traditions, my criticisms would be obvious and not particularly constructive. My dissatisfaction with what is largely silence regarding Mary in Protestant circles will be evident in later chapters.

Mary in Roman Catholicism

In 431 the Council of Ephesus declared that Mary was Theotokos, bearer or mother of God. This title, central to Roman Catholic (and Orthodox) understandings of Mary, emerged from vigorous debate concerning the relationship between the divine and human natures of Jesus. The Nestorians, who took their name from the Christian leader Nestorius, taught that Christ consisted of two distinct persons, God the Word and Jesus the human being. For them, therefore, Mary was the mother of the human Jesus but not the mother of God. The Council insisted, against the Nestorians, that the two natures of Christ form a single unity and that Mary is therefore rightly called the mother of God. To deny her that title is to deny Jesus' divinity. The title Theotokos, then, is first of all a christological assertion.

The Gospels of Matthew and Luke claim that Jesus was conceived without a human father, but already in the second century traditions arise that Mary remained a virgin when Jesus was born (see p. 103 below). The Fifth General Council in 553 makes this teaching official: Mary was a virgin when Jesus was conceived, she continued as a virgin even while giving birth, and indeed she remained a virgin throughout her life. The brothers and sisters of Jesus referred to in the New Testament were children of Joseph from an earlier marriage or perhaps they were even distant cousins.

In addition to these traditions regarding Mary's maternity and virginity, Roman Catholic reflection has concerned itself with the divine grace evident in Mary's life. In 1546 the Council of Trent insisted that she was entirely free of personal sin. And in 1854 Pius IX promulgated the dogma of the Immaculate Conception in *Ineffabilis Deus*. Long part of church tradition, the Immaculate Conception holds that Mary did not participate in original sin because she received sanctifying grace throughout her lifetime. This divine gift did not derive from Mary's own goodness or merit but was part of preparing her as an appropriate bearer for Jesus. Despite the misunderstandings that sometimes surround this teaching, the Immaculate Conception does not present Mary herself as having been born of a virgin; instead, it contends that she was the recipient of grace even before birth.

As the doctrine of the Immaculate Conception addresses the beginning of Mary's life, so the doctrine of the Assumption addresses its earthly ending. As the name suggests, the conviction here is that at the end of Mary's life, as the one human being perfectly redeemed by Jesus, she was assumed directly into heaven body and soul. In 1950 Pope Pius XII defined this teaching in the *Magnificantissimus Deus,* linking it directly to the Immaculate Conception.

Although never the subject of official doctrine and often of debate within the Catholic church itself, an important feature of Catholic thought regarding Mary concerns her role as "Mediatrix" or "Co-Redemptrix" alongside Christ. The language here is difficult, because it may seem to compromise the unique role of Christ as Mediator for humankind. In Catholic thought, however, Mary's mediation derives both from the communion of the saints and from her own standing. As the saints may intercede with God for the faithful on earth, Mary also may intercede, but Mary's unique role gives her mediation particular importance.

A notion that runs through much of Roman Catholic reflection on Mary, at least prior to the Second Vatican Council, is that Mary is aligned with Christ. She stands alongside Christ and facing the church, so that it is quite natural to think of Mary as having a role in redemption. This "christotypical" understanding of Mary does not end with Vatican II, but it is modified by a more "ecclesiotypical" approach. This approach, influenced by dramatic changes in Catholic biblical scholarship, understands Mary as standing with the church and facing Christ as one in need of redemption alongside the remainder of humanity. Most concretely, the strength of this newer understanding of Mary may be seen in the fact that Vatican II declined to issue a declaration devoted solely to Mary; instead, the role of Mary is discussed as the eighth chapter in *Lumen Gentium,* the council's document on the church.[27]

This very brief sketch of developments in official Catholic teaching should in no way be understood to assert uniformity in Roman Catholic thought. Two instances from ongoing discussions will illustrate the absence of unanimity. In Latin American circles the insights of liberation theology have offered renewed appreciation of Mary's identity with the poor and oppressed. In his ambitious treatment *The Maternal Face of God,* Leonardo Boff acknowledges the ways in which the Latin American base communities see the Magnificat in particular as a manifesto of prophecy and liberation.[28] Boff draws attention to the eschatological implications of Mary and her association with the Holy Spirit as a way of offering hope to oppressed people. More recently, Ivone Gebara and Maria C. Bingemer have undertaken to reinterpret traditional Marian teachings in ways that have particular relevance for Latin America.[29] For example, the virginal conception holds out the promise that, indeed, anything can happen, and the Immaculate Conception and Assumption affirm the goodness of bodily existence in a way that highlights the importance of life in the present. Along with this reinterpretation of official dogma in service of the people's needs, however, Gebara and Bingemer critically insist that church theology reckon with the "vital needs" of the poor that are "concealed in the pursuit of their mother Mary." For them, the "relationship with Mary, she who is 'alive in God,' full of affection and power, is direct: it is connected to the people's immediate and vital needs, since the life of the poor unfolds basically at this level."[30]

Feminists share many of the concerns of these liberation theologians, although on the whole they are more negative in their assessment of Marian traditions because of the perception that the veneration of Mary has served to reinforce sexist attitudes and behaviors.[31] Elisabeth Schüssler Fiorenza points out that most church teaching about Mary derives not from the New Testament but from a later patriarchal and clerically dominated church. She insists that feminists must articulate the harmful aspect of Marian teaching.[32] Rosemary Radford Ruether, while acknowledging the correlation between Marian teaching and the repression of women, works to retrieve from biblical tradition an image of Mary as representative of the church. For Ruether Mary's importance as representative of the church stems not from the fact that she is Jesus' mother but from her own obedience.[33] Elizabeth A. Johnson insists on the symbolic value of statements about Mary and anticipates a resymbolization of Mary's relationship to the church and believers.[34] Anne Carr provides an example of such a resymbolization when she proposes that a revised "fully human" understanding of Mary as one "who receives and communicates the grace of Christ in the Spirit corresponds with the description of the church as pilgrim."[35]

Liberation theology and feminist theology both emphasize the ecclesiotypical understanding of Mary that emerged from Vatican II. As important as that common feature is, it is also clear that Mary's place in the Roman Catholic church is under serious reappraisal at the present time.[36]

Mary in Orthodox Christianity

Mary occupies a place of singular importance in the life of Orthodox Christianity. Four major feasts commemorate major events in her life. Hundreds of hymns address her. Icons depicting Mary figure prominently in

Orthodox churches. In worship Orthodox Christians invoke Mary as "more honorable than the cherubim and beyond compare more glorious than the seraphim."

In spite of her iconographic prominence, Orthodox theologians have written relatively little about Mary. The reasons for this anomaly may be traced, somewhat paradoxically perhaps, to the prominence of Mary in worship; that is, Mary's prominence at the experiential level renders theological reflection either unnecessary or inadequate.[37] Nevertheless, Mary's importance in the thought of Orthodox Christianity may be gauged from the remark of Nikos Nissiotis: "There is *no Christian theology without continuous reference to the person and role of the Virgin Mary in the history of salvation.*"[38]

Those theologians who have written about Mary in recent decades have often been concerned to distinguish their understanding of Mary from that of Protestants, whose disregard of Mary they find inexplicable, and from that of Roman Catholics, in whom they see a tendency toward treating Mary as a theological category independent of christology.[39] In particular, Orthodox theologians reject the doctrine of the Immaculate Conception with its claim that Mary was conceived without original sin, largely because they hold to a different understanding of original sin, one that equates original sin with mortality. Mary was fully human, therefore subject to mortality and not exempt from original sin (although sinless herself). They similarly reject the Assumption because it appears to them to compromise the notion of Mary's mortality.[40]

Aside from these differences, the Orthodox understanding of Mary shares much with Roman Catholic teaching. In both traditions there is great emphasis on Mary as Theotokos, mother of God, and on Mary's perpetual virginity. Both also share an emphasis on correlating the role of Mary with that of Christ. What makes the Orthodox view of Mary distinctive is that, at the same time that Mary is regarded as Theotokos, the mother of God, she is also regarded as fully identified with humanity in all its weakness and mortality. Nissiotis, for example, speaks of securing Mary's place in *"the divine economy and within the Church community."*[41] A brief discussion of the two characteristic titles for Mary, Theotokos and Panhagia, will help to clarify this viewpoint.

Orthodox theologians emphasize that the title Theotokos must be understood christologically. That is to say, Mariology is not an independent category in systematic theology but an integral part of the theology of the incarnation (an insistence shared by Roman Catholic teaching since Vatican II). Neither is Mary's place in the incarnation merely that of a convenient vehicle, one whose service is complete when Jesus is born. Instead, she is "fully involved" as a "distinctive and elect person, sharing in the operation of giving birth to the hypostasis of the Logos as the unique personal revelation of God in history."[42] The bond created between the Theotokos and Christ is not severed at birth, but "continues *in the same degree* that the divine and human are inseparably united in Christ."[43] Thus, icons of the incarnation regularly depict both Mary and the infant Christ.

The central moment of the incarnation is the virgin birth. By means of the virginal conception, God reveals the futility of human notions of creativity and self-sufficiency. Quite apart from human biological processes or human intent or human generativity, Mary conceives. The incarnation comes about entirely by God's choice and by God's grace.[44]

At the same time, however, Orthodox theologians insist that Mary is deserving of this grace, and it is for that reason that she is identified as Panhagia, or All Holy. From birth she is without sin. Her own holiness and her divine maternity warrant the high veneration given her by the church. Mary is "the first of all humanity to have attained, through the complete transfiguration of her being, that to which every creature is summoned. She has already transcended the boundary between time and eternity and now finds herself in the Kingdom which the Church awaits with the second coming of Christ."[45] Because of Mary's own holiness, she stands in solidarity with the sanctified humanity who constitute the church. For this reason, Orthodox icons and hymns praise Mary at "the centre of the saints as a *representation of the worshipping and praying community.*"[46]

These two themes, the Theotokos which aligns Mary with the incarnate Logos and the Panhagia which aligns her with the church, stand in some tension with one another. By its insistence on affirming both simultaneously, Orthodox Christian tradition attempts to overcome what it sees as the deficiencies in both Roman Catholic and Protestant understandings of Mary.

Mary in Protestant Christianity

Although diversity of viewpoints among Protestants is virtually axiomatic, Protestant reflection on Mary (or the lack of Protestant reflection) does have certain regular features. First, the Protestant emphasis on biblical authority tends toward a reluctance to affirm more about Mary than can be found in the New Testament. Second, Protestant insistence on the centrality of christology means the rejection of any focus on Mary apart from Christ. Third, Protestants understand God's selection of Mary as entirely a result of divine grace, to the exclusion of any merit on her own part.

Karl Barth's treatment of Mary aptly illustrates all these features of Protestant reflection. Barth's discussion of Mary appears as part of his consideration of the virgin birth, that is, under the rubric of christology. He points to evidence in the New Testament for the virgin birth, although he concedes that many New Testament writings are silent on this issue. Despite the presence of the virgin birth in the New Testament, it actually makes its way into the church's creeds not by virtue of this historical witness but because of "a certain inward, essential rightness and importance in . . . connexion with the person of Jesus Christ."[47] For Barth what is at stake in the doctrine of the virgin birth is the mystery that "God stands at the start where real revelation takes place—God and not the arbitrary cleverness, capability, or piety of man."[48] In other words, Jesus' birth of a virgin demonstrates that sinful humankind possesses no "power, attribute or capacity" for God.[49] No human being wills Jesus into existence; all initiative comes from the side of God's gracious intervention.

To this point Barth appears to be in agreement with Orthodox teaching on Mary as described above, but he resists any discussion that threatens to attach an independent significance to Mary's gender or her person. Mary does not, either as representative of women or as an individual, merit her selection or demonstrate some capacity for cooperating with God. Instead, she is selected by God "to be conceiver of the eternal God Himself on earth."[50]

If Barth's position represents Protestant convention with respect to Mary, I see three variations on this convention that are broadly representative of Protestant thinking at present. The first, Protestant minimalism, can be illustrated in the work of Jürgen Moltmann. In his recent book, *The Way of Jesus Christ*, Moltmann undertakes a christology that is self-consciously developed within the context of the Jewish-Christian dialogue. He considers Mary only briefly and that in connection with what he refers to as "pneumatological christology."[51] Moltmann begins by observing the scanty nature of New Testament evidence regarding Mary. The doctrine of the virgin birth is not a "pillar" that supports the New Testament's claims regarding the incarnation: "The confession of faith in Jesus, the Son of God, the Lord, is independent of the virgin birth, and is not based on it."[52] For this reason Mariology is always sustained by christology and not the reverse: "It is for Christ's sake that his mother Mary is remembered and venerated."[53]

Emphasizing Matthew's and Luke's insistence that Jesus was conceived by the power of the Holy Spirit, Moltmann wishes to transfer much traditional Christian reflection on Mary to the person of the Holy Spirit. The Spirit then becomes "the great virginal, life-engendering mother of all the living, and as such the divine archetype of Mary, the mother of Jesus Christ."[54] It is to the Spirit, rather than to Mary, that Moltmann would look for the feminine side of God and the " 'motherly mystery' of the Trinity."[55] The result of this transposition from Mary to the Holy Spirit is that Mary becomes once more "the Jewish mother of Jesus." Any theological reflection on her significance, any Mariology, must take place as part of pneumatology.[56]

Moltmann's position is "conventionally" Protestant because of its stress on the pre-eminence of Scripture and its insistence that any role for Mary exists because of Christ and not the reverse. What makes Moltmann's position distinctive is his desire to preserve the roles Catholic tradition assigns to Mary but to transfer those roles from her to the Spirit.

If Moltmann represents Protestant minimalism, then Anglican theologian John Macquarrie represents a kind of Protestant maximalism. Macquarrie's 1990 volume, *Mary for All Christians,* attempts to reinterpret three classic Marian themes in ways that might be understood and appreciated by Protestants: the Immaculate Conception, the Assumption, and Mary as Corredemptrix.[57]

Macquarrie's approach can be illustrated by drawing on his discussion of the Immaculate Conception. Macquarrie understands the Immaculate Conception as referring not to a biological event but to "the absolute origination of a person."[58] In this sense, Mary's conception occurs first within the mind of God; that is, "in the beginning God had elected Mary to her unique vocation in the scheme of salvation."[59] In the same way, the entirety of humankind is included within the realm of God's election, but Mary has a specific role in connection with what Paul so elegantly refers to as "the fullness of time." Mary's conception also takes place within the context of Israel, the people with whom God entered into covenant and who had the task of preparing the way for Jesus Christ. Finally, Mary's conception occurs within the context of the marriage of her parents, whom tradition refers to as Anna and Joachim. That conception is biological, of course, but Macquarrie wisely notes that it is also personal and spiritual. In this larger sense of the Immaculate Conception, Macquarrie contends, the doctrine does not threaten the Protestant insistence on salvation by grace alone but indeed enhances it, for it demonstrates that the "favor" shown to Mary (Luke 1:28) results from God's larger plan for the salvation of humankind.[60]

As Moltmann represents one convention within Protestantism, so Macquarrie represents another, that of the ecumenical movement. Particularly for Christians who are involved in ecumenical discussions, the need to find and claim common ground with other Christians sparks a willingness to listen to the language of other traditions (e.g., the Immaculate Conception) and reinterpret that language in ways congenial to one's own traditions.

A third Protestant approach, that of Protestant feminism, is probably best represented by the Episcopal bishop John Shelby Spong in his book *Born of a Woman.*[61] It is difficult to determine to what extent Spong's views are representative. It is also awkward to draw on Spong, who admits that he writes a popularization that leans heavily on the works of biblical scholars such as Raymond E. Brown and Jane Schaberg. Precisely because the book has received considerable attention in the press, however, it may be important to attend to it.

The conclusion of Spong that has captured widespread attention is that Marian teaching has been harmful to women. This notion by no means originates with Spong, of course, but he has put it sharply and publicly: "The figure of the virgin has in fact been employed as a male weapon to repress women by defining them in the name of a God called Father, to be less human than males, to be the source of a sexual desire that was thought to be evil, and therefore to be guilty just for being women."[62]

In his final chapter, entitled "The Cost of the Virgin Myth," Spong reiterates that the "idea" of the virgin Mary has had disastrous consequences for women. "The only hope for the survival of the virgin Mary as a viable symbol is her redefinition by the new consciousness."[63]

What should be most startling about the three Protestant positions I have sketched is that all are represented by male writers—even that of Protestant feminism. To date, I have identified only a few Protestant women who have written about Mary,[64] and they have written sermons or meditations rather than scholarly articles or monographs; that is to say, they address the questions conventionally associated with Mary devotionally rather than systematically. At present the best explanation I can offer for this silence is that Protestant women have worked under the same resistance to talk about Mary that characterizes the theology of Protestant men. Many Protestants still find any discourse about Mary uncomfortable. I also suspect that Protestant women who see the controversy about Mary among Roman Catholic women may remove themselves from what they perceive as the "territory" of their sisters.

THE LITERARY QUEST FOR MARY

The theological quest for Mary begins with the biblical texts but quickly moves beyond them to construct an understanding of Mary and her place in the larger framework of God's dealings with humankind. The historical quest begins with the biblical texts but looks behind them for any historical data they might yield about Mary and the individuals or communities who produced the Gospels themselves. What I undertake in this study is, by contrast, a literary quest.[65] Although many previous studies of Mary contain insights of a literary nature, and I have benefited significantly from those, I am not aware of a study that does what I intend. I am interested in the ways in which these writers portray Mary as a literary character and the roles she plays in their narratives. Rather than looking "behind" or "beyond" the text,

I am concerned with the text itself, the way it works, the world it creates. The "glimpses" of Mary I seek, therefore, are primarily literary rather than theological or historical.

Readers who are accustomed to see the Bible as a collection of historical information may find this approach unusual. I select it because I believe the historical quest sketched earlier in this chapter has yielded all that it can, at least in the absence of further discoveries of ancient texts or material remains. In common with a number of biblical scholars, I also am convinced that, in the rush to read behind narratives for their historical value, scholars have often slighted the story in and of itself.[66]

I characterize my treatment as "primarily" literary, since some historical questions will inevitably arise. For example, how would a first-century reader have understood the Greek word *parthenos,* usually translated into English as "virgin"? And, since any study of early Christian texts as literature involves questions about the overall goal of the text or its "governing principle," questions of theology will be close to hand. However, I make no effort to assess the historicity of these narratives or to construct a life of Mary. Neither do I propose a theological interpretation of Mary's place in the church.

The primary questions to be addressed here have to do with the ways in which early Christian writers portray Mary as a character and the role or roles she plays in their re-presentations of the Jesus story. While the desirability of studying characterization within early Christian texts, particularly the Gospels, may seem obvious, characterization itself has, until recently, received relatively little attention either in biblical studies or in secular literary criticism. The well-known quotation from Aristotle about characters existing to serve plot and E. M. Forster's distinction between flat and round characters summarized the bulk of critical reflection on the issue of character.[67] The past two decades, however, have witnessed a growing discussion of the elusive phenomenon of characterization.[68] Among the more suggestive discussions is that of Mary Doyle Springer, whose study of women in the novels of Henry James begins with the following definition of character:

> A literary character is an artificial construct drawn from, and relatively imitative of, people in the real world. The identity of a character becomes known primarily from a continuity of his or her own choices, speeches, and acts, consistent with the kind of person to be presented. Secondarily, identity is reinforced by description, diction, and in incidents of apposition to other characters. The choices, acts, and habits that constitute a character are limited by, consistent with, and suitable to the governing principle of the whole work of which the character is a part. The

"life" of a literary character thus comes to a close when his or
her part in the work is complete.[69]

A close examination of this definition will provide a number of helpful
clues for the study of Mary. First, character is an "artificial construct."
While literary characters necessarily are imitative of "real" people, else the
reader would find them unintelligible, literary characters are also necessarily
"artificial." Even when we read treatments of historical figures, we encounter an invention of the author. The vast array of biographical treatments of
John F. Kennedy should make this point clear; in each of those treatments
we encounter the author's understanding of Kennedy, a construct that is
never more than an approximation of the "real" Kennedy.

Similarly, in Mark's Gospel the Jesus whom we encounter is not the
equivalent of the historical figure, a person who slept and ate and perhaps
even discussed daily affairs such as the weather and the difficulty of family
life. Mark presents us with his interpretation of Jesus, an interpretation that
is, however powerful kerygmatically or didactically, also a product of
Mark's art. It is, in that sense, "artificial."[70]

An illustration drawn from Kenneth Clark's study of the nude in art
helps to clarify this point. Clark comments that the nude is an art "invented
by the Greeks": "It is widely supposed that the naked human body is in
itself an object upon which the eye dwells with pleasure and which we are
glad to see depicted. But anyone who has frequented art schools and seen
the shapeless, pitiful models that the students are industriously drawing will
know that this is an illusion. The body is not one of those subjects which
can be made into art by direct transcription. . . . In almost every detail the
body is not the shape that art has led us to believe it should be."[71] If even
the careful depiction of a human model sitting in the artist's presence invariably creates or invents that figure, then the literary depiction of character is
also necessarily an invention.

This invention or artificial construct, the character, becomes known to
the reader in a variety of ways, primary among which are the choices made
by the character. Already in Aristotle the point is made that the most basic
thing that a character "must do in order to emerge as a character is to be seen
to make a choice."[72] However lean or full the description of a character, that
description needs the confirmation or disconfirmation of the character's action. Perhaps nowhere in Ishiguro's poignant novel, *The Remains of the
Day,* does the reader learn more about Mr. Stevens's dignified sense of duty
than in the brief scene in which the butler chooses to continue service at a
dinner party moments after the death of his father.[73]

Characters are also revealed through speech, actions, and description,
according to Springer. Robert Alter's discussion of the ways in which char-

acters are revealed in biblical texts helpfully amplifies Springer's definition: "Character can be revealed through the report of actions, through appearance, gestures, posture, costume; through one character's comments on another; through direct speech by the character; through inward speech, either summarized or quoted as interior monologue; or through statements by the narrator about the attitudes and intentions of the personages, which may come either as flat assertions or motivated explanations."[74]

If we are inclined to isolate characters from their narrative homes, Springer's definition reminds us that characters emerge in contrast with other characters. "Characters, then, can serve to reveal *other* characters—to make, by their own choices and acts, rhetorical judgments on the choices and acts of others. . . . Wherever there are two or more characters there is a 'dramatic situation' of some kind where *interaction* reveals character, or where the mere juxtaposition of characters reveals character. . . ." In order to alter our sense of them, characters do not even need to meet, but only to appear within one "coherent fiction."[75]

All of the presentation of a character is, in Springer's words, suitable to the "governing principle of the whole work of which the character is a part." Baruch Hochman insists that characters "mean something" as "part of a configuration of meaning that the work as a whole articulates."[76] These observations are, at one level, so obvious as to seem ridiculous; what sense would it make if a character were *unsuitable* for the work as a whole? What Springer and Hochman identify, however, becomes crucially important for any investigation of characterization in a Gospel narrative; since the evangelists clearly wrote to promote a certain understanding of Jesus, a goal that is theological in some sense, characters exist to serve that goal rather than simply to draw attention to themselves or to entertain the reader.

Springer's definition itself supplies us with questions that may be carried into our reading of the narratives in which Mary plays a part. Two further points need to be made at the outset, however. One is that character emerges as a narrative develops. Even with authors such as Jane Austen or Anthony Trollope, who often introduce characters by means of elaborate portraits, the readers nevertheless come to know the characters more fully as the story develops.[77] That observation requires that a study of Mary likewise attend to the way she functions *as each story progresses*.

I emphasize this point, which would be obvious in reading literature outside the Bible, because the dominant historical analysis of biblical texts has dealt less with the progressive development of narrative than with the historicity of individual passages. As a result, for example, the scene that brings the Lukan infancy narrative to a conclusion (2:41–52) has not been treated as an integral part of the narrative that begins in 1:5 but as a later addition that reveals little of Luke's perspective.[78] By contrast, when I take up Luke's Gospel in chapter 3, I shall be concerned with the difference between Mary's response to the angel Gabriel in 1:38 and her apparent lack of understanding at Luke 2:48 and 50.

A second issue to be addressed at the outset is that Mary is, at least in the canonical narratives if not in the Protevangelium, a minor character. Even in the Gospel of Luke, where she appears more often than anywhere else in the New Testament, she is scarcely present beyond the opening chapters. That fact makes a study of the characterization of Mary different from studies of the characterization of Jesus, for example, or of the Jewish leaders. Even minor characters, however, have important functions in narrative. Springer describes secondary or minor characters as those "whose function is nevertheless necessary or highly desirable to the affective power of the work as a whole [even though they are secondary]. These tend to change minimally, or to remain static, and serve as complements to the primary characters."[79]

This discussion of characterization in literature suggests several questions that will govern our reading of the narratives in the following chapters:

> What does Mary say and do?
> How do other characters speak to and about her? What actions do they take that have significance for her?
> How is Mary described in comparison and contrast with other characters?
> In what ways, if any, does Mary change as the narrative develops?
> What role or roles does Mary play in the development of the plot?
> What place does Mary have in the "governing principle" of the work itself?

Various historical quests for Mary concern themselves with identifying the contours of her life or the development of traditions about her. And various theological quests undertake to define her relationship to God and Jesus, on the one hand, and to the church, on the other. In the chapters that follow, by contrast, we seek to understand the characterization of Mary in four early Christian narratives, her place in those stories.

NOTES

1. Ode 19:11, trans. J. H. Charlesworth, in *The Old Testament Pseudepigrapha*, ed. J. H. Charlesworth (2 vols.; Garden City, N.Y.: Doubleday, 1983, 1985) 2:753.
2. The poems are entitled, "the astrologer predicts at Mary's birth," "anna speaks of the childhood of mary her daughter," "mary's dream" [see below, p. 49],

"how he is coming then," "holy night," "a song of mary," and "island mary," and may be found in Clifton's collection *two-headed woman* (Amherst: University of Massachusetts Press, 1980) 34–41.

3. *Death Comes for the Archbishop* (New York: Vintage Books, 1971 [1927]) 216.

4. Here I rely upon the theory of Markan priority, which holds that Mark wrote the first of the Gospels known to us and that Matthew and Luke, independently of one another, rely upon Mark in addition to other sources and their own editing or redactions. Although recent decades have witnessed a reconsideration of this issue, in my judgment Markan priority still provides the best account we have of the literary relationships among the synoptic Gospels.

5. See the extended discussion of this question in John P. Meier, *A Marginal Jew: Rethinking the Historical Jesus*, vol. 1: *The Roots of the Problem and the Person* (New York: Doubleday, 1991) 318–32.

6. See the helpful discussion of this issue in Bernadette J. Brooten, "Jewish Women's History in the Roman Period: A Task for Christian Theology," in *Christians among Jews and Gentiles*, ed. George W. E. Nickelsburg with George W. MacRae, S.J. (Philadelphia: Fortress, 1986) 22–30.

7. *The Mishnah*, trans. Herbert Danby (Oxford: Oxford University Press, 1933) 752.

8. *Her Share of the Blessings: Women's Religions among Pagans, Jews, and Christians in the Greco-Roman World* (New York: Oxford University Press, 1992) 93.

9. *Philo*, vol. IX: *Flaccus*, trans. F. H. Colson (LCL; Cambridge: Harvard University Press, 1941) 350–51.

10. See the evidence collected by Ross S. Kraemer in "Jewish Women in the Diaspora World of Late Antiquity," in *Jewish Women in Historical Perspective*, ed. Judith R. Baskin (Detroit: Wayne State University Press, 1991) 45–46.

11. *The Mishnah*, 250.

12. *Corpus Papyrorum Judaicarum*, 144. This papyrus is readily available in Ross S. Kraemer, ed., *Maenads, Martyrs, Matrons, Monastics: A Sourcebook on Women's Religions in the Greco-Roman World* (Philadelphia: Fortress, 1988) 88; see also the discussion in Kraemer, "Jewish Women in the Diaspora," 58. Although the papyrus does not identify either the man or the woman as Jewish, it was found in a collection of ancient Jewish documents.

13. *The Documents from the Bar Kokhba Period in the Cave of Letters: Greek Papyri*, ed. Naphtali Lewis (Judean Desert Studies, vol. 2; Jerusalem: Israel Exploration Society, 1989).

14. *The Mishnah*, 322.

15. *The Babylonian Talmud*, vol. 3, Part 8: *Kiddushin* (London: Soncino, 1936) 141.

16. Daniel Boyarin, *Carnal Israel: Reading Sex in Talmudic Culture* (Berkeley: University of California Press, 1993) especially 25–30, 167–96.

17. *Women Leaders in the Ancient Synagogue* (Brown Judaic Studies, 36; Chico, Calif.: Scholars, 1982).

18. Ibid.; see also Kraemer, "Jewish Women in the Diaspora," 48–49.

19. Ed. Raymond E. Brown, Karl P. Donfried, Joseph A. Fitzmyer, and John Reumann (Philadelphia: Fortress, 1978). Brown's masterful volume *The Birth of the Messiah* (updated edition; New York: Doubleday, 1993) figures prominently in the chapters below and might well be discussed alongside or instead of *Mary in the New Testament*. Because the latter volume is multi-authored and thus reflects the judgments of several scholars from differing perspectives, I have chosen to employ it here as representative of the historical approach.

20. See below, p. 71–72, for my discussion of this passage, where I argue that the reference to Mary in Acts 1:14 serves an important literary and theological function for Luke.

21. *The Illegitimacy of Jesus: A Feminist Theological Interpretation of the Infancy Narratives* (San Francisco: Harper and Row, 1987).

22. *The Liberation of Christmas: The Infancy Narratives in Social Context* (New York: Crossroad, 1989).

23. Ibid., 19.

24. Ibid., 9.

25. "Mother and Son," *BTB* 20 (1990) 54–64. Additional articles in the same issue of this journal explore the significance of Mary as a Mediterranean woman for understanding the theological significance of Mary's virginity, her portrayal in art and literature, the occurrence of Marian apparitions, and devotion to Mary.

26. Ibid., 63.

27. See the helpful discussion in Tambasco, *What Are They Saying About Mary?* (New York: Paulist, 1984), especially 3–11, and the summary of the workings of Vatican II in Alberic Stacpoole, OSB, "Mary's Place in *Lumen Gentium, Vatican II's Constitution on the Church," in Mary and the Churches,* ed. Alberic Stacpoole, OSB (Dublin: Columba Press, 1987) 85–97.

28. Trans. Robert R. Barr and John W. Diercksmeier (San Francisco: Harper and Row, 1987).

29. *Mary: Mother of God, Mother of the Poor,* trans. Phillip Berryman (Maryknoll, N.Y.: Orbis, 1989).

30. Ibid., 126.

31. For a helpful survey of these discussions, see Els Maeckelberghe, *Desperately Seeking Mary: A Feminist Appropriation of a Traditional Religious Symbol* (Kampen, The Netherlands: Kok Pharos, 1991) 7–42.

32. "Feminist Theology as a Critical Theology of Liberation," *TS* 36 (1975) 605–626.

33. *Mary: The Feminine Face of the Church* (Philadelphia: Westminster, 1977).

34. "The Symbolic Character of Theological Statements about Mary," *JES* 22 (1985) 312–35; "The Marian Tradition and the Reality of Women," *Horizons* 12 (1985) 116–35.

35. "Mary: Model of Faith," in *Mary, Woman of Nazareth: Biblical and Theological Perspectives,* ed. Doris Donnelly (New York: Paulist, 1989) 20.

36. The literature on Mary in Roman Catholic thought seems limitless. A good place to begin further reading is with Anthony J. Tambasco, *What Are They Saying About Mary?,* while Karl Rahner's *Mary: Mother of the Lord* (New York:

Herder and Herder, 1963) provides an elegant and compact explanation of key doctrines. For a more extensive history of Marian doctrine, see Hilda Graef, *Mary: A History of Doctrine and Devotion* (2 vols.; London: Sheed and Ward, 1963, 1965).

37. Nikos Nissiotis, "Mary in Orthodox Theology," *Mary in the Churches*, ed. Hans Küng and Jürgen Moltmann (Edinburgh: T. and T. Clark, 1983) 25.
38. Ibid.
39. Georges Florovsky, "The Ever-Virgin Mother of God," in *The Collected Works of Georges Florovsky,* vol 3: *Creation and Redemption* (Belmont, Mass.: Nordland, 1976) 173.
40. Hilda Graef, *Mary,* 2:130–33.
41. Nissiotis, "Mary in Orthodox Theology," 26.
42. Ibid.
43. Sergius Bulgakov, *The Orthodox Church* (Crestwood, N.Y.: St. Vladimir's Seminary Press, 1988) 117 (italics mine).
44. Nissiotis, "Mary in Orthodox Theology," 30–31.
45. Leonid Ouspensky, *Theology of the Icon: Volume I,* trans. Anthony Gythiel (Crestwood, N.Y.: St. Vladimir's Seminary Press, 1992) 60.
46. Nissiotis, "Mary in Orthodox Theology," 26.
47. Karl Barth, *Church Dogmatics,* vol. 1, pt. 2: *Doctrine of the Word of God,* ed. G. W. Bromiley and T. F. Torrance (Edinburgh: T. and T. Clark, 1956) 176.
48. Ibid., 182.
49. Ibid., 188.
50. Ibid., 196.
51. *The Way of Jesus Christ: Christology in Messianic Dimensions,* trans. Margaret Kohl (San Francisco: HarperSanFrancisco, 1990) 73.
52. Ibid., 79.
53. Ibid., 80.
54. Ibid., 84.
55. Ibid., 86.
56. Ibid.
57. *Mary for All Christians* (Grand Rapids: Eerdmans, 1990).
58. Ibid., 62.
59. Ibid., 63.
60. Ibid., 73–76.
61. *Born of a Woman: A Bishop Rethinks the Birth of Jesus* (San Francisco: HarperSanFrancisco, 1992).
62. Ibid., 198.
63. Ibid., 224.
64. This question is complicated because library catalogues and periodical indexes do not indicate the gender or denominational affiliation of authors. Generally speaking, however, books and articles on Mary will include some reference to the author's tradition.
65. What I have termed the "historical" quest is also a form of literary study, as Meir Sternberg would insist (*The Poetics of Biblical Narrative: Ideological Lit-*

erature and the Drama of Reading [Bloomington: Indiana University Press, 1985] 7–23). Sternberg helpfully distinguishes between literary approaches that are concerned with source (i.e., the history of the text or behind the text) and those concerned with discourse (i.e., the workings of the text itself). In biblical studies, the distinction of historical from literary approaches has become conventional, however, and I follow it here even if it is somewhat misleading.

66. The book that marks the re-introduction of literary criticism into New Testament scholarship is R. Alan Culpepper's landmark study, *Anatomy of the Fourth Gospel* (Philadelphia: Fortress, 1983). A readable introduction to central issues is found in Mark Allan Powell, *What Is Narrative Criticism?* (Minneapolis: Fortress, 1990). An important entry to the burgeoning bibliography is found in Mark Allan Powell, ed., *The Bible and Modern Literary Criticism* (Bibliographies and Indexes in Religious Studies 22; New York: Greenwood, 1992).

67. *Aristotle's Poetics,* trans. Leon Golden, commentary by O. B. Harbison (Tallahassee: University Presses of Florida, 1981) 1450a–b; E. M. Forster, *Aspects of the Novel* (New York: Harcourt Brace Jovanovich, 1955) 65–82.

68. One hotly contested issue at the center of the discussion of character is to what extent characters may be discussed apart from their narrative contexts; are they so embedded in texts as to be inseparable from them, or do they acquire sufficient contours in the course of a story that they in some sense become independent from the story? Because this study will focus precisely on Mary's place *within a particular set of narratives,* this theoretical question becomes somewhat peripheral. For a concise statement of the question, see Shlomith Rimmon-Kenan, *Narrative Fiction: Contemporary Poetics* (London: Methuen, 1983) 31–34; Baruch Hochman's *Character in Literature* carefully considers the strengths of the formalist position, while insisting nevertheless on the independence of fictional character (Ithaca: Cornell University Press, 1985).

69. *A Rhetoric of Literary Character: Some Women of Henry James* (Chicago: University of Chicago Press, 1978) 14. I am grateful to C. Clifton Black for drawing my attention to Springer's work and to this paragraph in particular; see his discussion in "Depth of Characterization and Degrees of Faith in Matthew," *Society of Biblical Literature Seminar Papers 1989,* ed. David J. Lull (SBLSPS 28; Atlanta: Scholars, 1989) 604–23.

70. Those familiar with the history of biblical scholarship will recognize in this comment a parallel to the distinction between the Jesus of history and the Christ of faith.

71. *The Nude: A Study in Ideal Form* (New York: Pantheon, 1956) 4–7; quoted in Martin Price, *Forms of Life: Character and Moral Imagination in the Novel* (New Haven: Yale University Press, 1983) 37–38.

72. Springer, *Rhetoric of Literary Character,* 32. The relevant passages in Aristotle are 2.1.11 and 2.1.9–13 in *The Eudemian Ethics,* trans. H. Rackham (LCL; Cambridge; Harvard University Press, 1935) 240–41, 304–307.

73. Kazuo Ishiguro, *The Remains of the Day* (New York: Vintage International, 1989) 106.

74. *The Art of Biblical Narrative* (New York: Basic Books, 1981) 116–17.

75. *Rhetoric of Literary Character,* 191–92.
76. *Character in Literature,* 66.
77. James Phelan, *Reading People, Reading Plots: Character, Progression and the Interpretation of Narrative* (Chicago: University of Chicago Press, 1989) 15.
78. See the helpful discussion of the importance of sequence for characterization in John A. Darr, *On Character Building: The Reader and the Rhetoric of Characterization in Luke-Acts* (Louisville: Westminster, 1992) 42–43.
79. *Rhetoric of Literary Character,* 14.

CHAPTER 2

Threatened and Threatening

Mary in the Gospel of Matthew

It is a heart,
This holocaust I walk in,
O golden child the world will kill and eat.
Sylvia Plath,"Mary's Song"

With these haunting lines Sylvia Plath imagines Mary's terror-stricken anticipation of both the crucifixion of Jesus and the holocaust of European Jewry. "Mary's Song" seems a particularly fitting introduction to our investigation of Mary's treatment in Matthew's Gospel. Although she does not speak in this narrative, much less sing, she does play a role in the foreshadowing of the crucifixion.

One contemporary commentary on Matthew carries the subtitle, "The Teacher's Gospel,"[1] but glimpses of Mary within this "teacher's gospel" are exceedingly slender. Her name appears in the genealogy of Jesus (1:16), and her pregnancy is the subject of the first dream in which an angel speaks to Joseph (1:18–25). She appears at several points in the remainder of the "birth narrative." During the account of Jesus' ministry, Matthew mentions her only twice. In a scene paralleling Luke 8:19–21 and Mark 3:31–35, she comes to speak to Jesus (12:46–50), and in 13:53–58 her name is mentioned as Jesus returns home and the locals try to puzzle out the nature of their neighbor's strength and wisdom. Whatever the aims of Matthew's teaching gospel, the curriculum devotes scant space to Mary.

Following the plan sketched in the preceding chapter, the task here will be to understand Matthew's portrayal of Mary. To anticipate, I shall argue that Matthew's characterization of Mary consists entirely of positioning her within the genealogy (in Matthew 1) and alongside the infant Jesus (in Matthew 2). Like Jesus, Mary poses a threat and is threatened in return. Like Jesus also, divine intervention delivers her.

THE ORIGINS OF THE MESSIAH JESUS
(MATTHEW 1:1–2:23)

The contrasts with the well-known first two chapters of Luke dominate our initial reading of Matthew 1–2. Although Luke may be said to begin his Gospel with a birth narrative, because he narrates not only the events preceding Jesus' birth but also the circumstances of the birth and various responses to it, Matthew's account scarcely even mentions the birth itself (2:1). Matthew begins with a genealogy, seems to highlight the importance of Joseph (although see below, p. 43, on the place of Joseph in Matthew's story), introduces both the visiting magi and King Herod, includes the story of the flight to Egypt and the slaughter of Bethlehem's infants, locates the home of Joseph and Mary in Bethlehem rather than Nazareth, and interprets the entire story by means of a series of quotations from the Old Testament. Nowhere in this version of Jesus' origins do we learn of a family relationship between Jesus and John the Baptist, an angelic annunciation to Mary or her responses to events, the visit of shepherds, or even one trip to Jerusalem. All that belongs to Luke. While the two stories agree at points, they are quite simply that—two different stories.

Comparisons between these two accounts are customary and perhaps even unavoidable, but they should not prevent us from taking Matthew's story on its own terms. Even if we rightly label Luke 1:5–2:52 a birth narrative, it is a mistake to assign Matthew 1:1–2:23 to the same category. Instead of a birth narrative, we might term Matthew's an account of the *origins* of Jesus Christ in which he connects Jesus with the history of Israel. As such, Matthew's story concentrates on the genealogy of Jesus, his relationship to Joseph, and the various ways in which Jesus' birth fulfills biblical prophecy.

An earlier generation of scholars viewed the Matthean account of Jesus' origins as a collection of independent stories rather than a unified account. Recent study, however, has emphasized the internal unity of Matthew 1 and the internal unity of Matthew 2, if not always their interrelatedness. In a classic essay, "Quis et Unde?," Krister Stendahl argued that the two issues dominating Matthew's infancy narrative are "Who?"*(Quis)* and "Whence?" *(Unde)*. Chapter 1 of Matthew explains who Jesus is, and chapter 2 describes the itinerary of the infant Jesus through locations that carry significant theological weight (Bethlehem, Egypt, Ramah).[2] Raymond E. Brown has further refined this scheme by adding to the questions "Who?" and "Whence?" the questions "How?" and "Whither?" In chapter 1 of the Gospel, Brown argues, Matthew demonstrates not only *that* Jesus is Son of David but *how* that may be said to be the case. Chapter 2 explains not only where Jesus was born but also where his life and ministry will lead him (i.e., into hostility).[3] On this reading, the structure of Matthew 1–2 would be:

Part 1	Who?	1:1–17	Genealogy
	How?	1:18–25	Conception of Jesus
Part 2	Whence?	2:1–12	Coming of the magi to Jerusalem
	Whither?	2:13–23	Flight to Egypt and return to Nazareth

This analysis shows that each of the two halves of this story (chapter 1 and chapter 2) is tightly knit together, but it neglects the ways in which the two halves parallel each other. Each half begins with reference to the birth of Jesus (1:1, 2:1). English translations generally obscure the relationship between the term *genesis* ("genealogy" in NRSV) in 1:1 and the verb *gennān* ("was born" in NRSV) in 2:1, but these come from the same Greek root. Matthew 1:1 refers to the birth record of Jesus and 2:1 to the fact of his birth.[4]

Each half of this narrative of Jesus' origins also ends with a similar motif:

And he named him [lit., "called his name"] Jesus.
(1:25)

He will be called a Nazorean. (2:23)

In both cases the identification of Jesus' name completes some aspect of the story. The angel commands Joseph to give the child the name Jesus (1:21), so that the naming indicates Joseph's compliance as well as divine intention. Similarly, the movement of Joseph to Nazareth rather than Bethlehem, again at the direction of the angel, is said to fulfill a prophecy concerning the Messiah (2:23).[5]

Not only do the two parts of the narrative begin and end in parallel fashion, but they also have a common dynamic. In each part some serious threat pervades the story. Here I anticipate several points that need further elaboration, but it will be helpful to introduce this particular parallel here. In the first half of the narrative Joseph poses a threat to Mary (and, by implication, to Jesus as well), just as circumstances have threatened several significant women in Israel's history (and, by implication, their offspring and the line of David). In the second half of the narrative Herod poses a threat to the infant Jesus (and, by implication, also to Mary). Each agent who threatens Mary and Jesus wishes to act in secret (1:19, 2:7). Joseph is a character who acts out of motivations that are (apparently) good and Herod out of evil motivations, but they alike threaten God's plan and must be stopped.

If we take into account these similar features of the two halves of the narrative, then a revised analysis of the structure of Matthew 1–2 emerges:

Part I		Part II	
1:1–17	Birth record of Jesus (Threats to the line implied along the way)	2:1–12	Birth of Jesus brings magi (Threat to Jesus implied along the way)
1:18–25	Threat to Mary Conception of Jesus God resolves threat Name of Jesus	2:13–23	Threat to Jesus Flight to Egypt God resolves threat Name of Jesus

As we examine Matthew's characterization of Mary, the parallels between these two parts of the narrative of Jesus' origins will emerge more clearly.

The Birth Record of Jesus

In the most general sense, 1:1 states the purpose of the genealogy of 1:1–17; it records the birth of Jesus Christ *as* son of David and son of Abraham. That is, in order to show who Jesus is, Matthew gives an account of Jesus' ancestors in the line of David. Numerous historical problems appear in this genealogy, which more accurately reflects Matthew's theology than it does any historical accounting in the modern sense of the term *history*.[6] In conformity with a style found in Old Testament genealogies, the genealogy consists of a chain of statements with the form, "X begat [or "was the father of" NRSV] Y" (cf., e.g., 1 Chron 1:13). As has long been recognized, however, Matthew occasionally departs from this convention. These departures from the usual genealogical form not only reveal something of Matthew's understanding of Jesus but also Matthew's understanding of Mary.

Matthew alters the expected genealogical pattern at the following points:

1:2   Jacob begat *Judah and his brothers*
1:3   Judah begat *Perez and Zerah from Tamar*
1:5   Salmon begat Boaz *from Rahab*
1:5   Boaz begat Obed *from Ruth*
1:6   Jesse begat David *the King*

1:6   David begat Solomon *from the wife of Uriah*

1:11   Josiah begat *Jechoniah and his brothers, at the time of the deportation to Babylon*

1:12   *After the deportation to Babylon* Jechoniah begat Shealtiel

1:16   Jacob begat Joseph *the husband of Mary, from whom was begotten Jesus, the one called Christ.*

(author's translation)

Since the genealogy ends with a division of the list into three periods of time (Abraham to David, David to the exile, and the exile to Christ), references to David as "the King" and to the deportation probably stand in the list as indicators of those very divisions. The reference to Jechoniah and his brothers at the time of the Babylonian exile may serve as a further reminder of those who were deported; that is, not an individual but an entire community is deported. Identification of Jacob's children as "Judah and his brothers" underscores the unity and importance of that group of twelve, the significance of which appears again later in Matthew's Gospel. The inclusion of both Perez and Zerah presumably occurs because they are twins. (For the time being, I defer discussion of the reference to Mary, because this final alteration in the genealogical form will be discussed at length below. See pp. 39–40.)

Having identified certain of these deviations as something like road signs within the text, we are left with the names of the four women and two sons of one of those women:

1:3   Judah begat Perez and Zerah *from Tamar*

1:5   Salmon begat Boaz *from Rahab*

1:5   Boaz begat Obed *from Ruth*

1:6   David begat Solomon *from the wife of Uriah.*

While the inclusion of women in genealogies is rare in the Hebrew Bible, it does occur, especially in contexts where the writer lists all the male descendants of an individual and attempts to distinguish among the sons born to various wives or concubines of the same man (e.g., Gen 11:29–30, 35:22–26; 1 Chron 2:18–21). But Matthew's genealogy is a linear one, limited to direct paternal descent, and thus the appearance of women's names is unexpected. And, to heighten the startling character of these additions, the women whose names appear are not Sarah and Rebecca and Rachel, but women whose stories teem with ambiguity and impropriety. Attention to each of them will enhance our consideration of the various explanations of their presence in Matthew's genealogy and, in turn, shed light on the fifth woman in the genealogy, Mary.

Tamar, the first woman in Matthew's genealogy, did indeed become the mother of Perez and Zerah through Judah, but the story is a complex one, fraught with much irony. The story appears in Genesis 38 immediately following the selling of Joseph by his brothers. Judah, who takes an active role in depriving his father of Joseph, abruptly leaves the brothers and marries a Canaanite woman.[7] The couple produces three sons, and Judah eventually secures Tamar as a wife for the eldest, Er. Er dies as a result of divine punishment for his own (unspecified) wickedness, and Judah sends the second son, Onan, to marry Tamar, in keeping with levirate marriage customs. Onan also dies as a result of God's judgment, because Onan practices *coitus interruptus* rather than father a child for his dead brother (see Deut 25:5–10). Out of fear for the life of his third son, Shelah, Judah returns Tamar to her father's house, promising to send for her when Shelah is of marriageable age.

When time passes and Tamar has not been recalled to the household of Judah as wife of Shelah, she knows that she has been wronged by her father-in-law, who is obliged to assist her. Hearing that Judah is nearby, Tamar removes her widow's garments, veils herself, and sits at the entrance to Enaim so that Judah must see her. Seeing her at the roadside and with covered face, Judah, now a widower himself, assumes that Tamar is a prostitute and negotiates for her services. As security for the kid Judah promises to give her, Tamar takes Judah's signet, cord, and staff—unmistakable signs of his identity.

Judah later commissions a friend to deliver the promised kid, but the friend fails to find the "prostitute" and learns that there is no prostitute at Enaim (as indeed there is not!). Fearing ridicule, Judah does not pursue the matter further, allowing the "prostitute" to keep his signet, cord, and staff. Eventually Judah learns that his daughter-in-law is pregnant and he summarily pronounces: "Bring her out, and let her be burned" (Gen 38:24). But Tamar responds by sending the signet and cord and staff to Judah, with the comment that the owner of these items is also the father of her child. Judah acknowledges possession of the items: "She is more in the right than I, since I did not give her to my son Shelah" (Gen 38:26). The sons born of this pregnancy are Perez and Zerah.

Tamar appears to be a prostitute, but in fact she is not; she acts only to secure for herself what is due her. Rahab, however, the second woman in the Matthean genealogy, is indeed a prostitute. In the story of the conquest of Jericho, the spies Joshua sends to Jericho secure lodging in Rahab's house for reasons that are left unstated (Joshua 2). When the agents of the king of Jericho attempt to find the men, Rahab hides them and tells the king's men that the spies left the city before the gates were closed for the evening. She then goes to the roof, where she had earlier hidden the spies, and seeks from them a promise of protection during the upcoming siege of Jericho, acknowledging that Yahweh's sponsorship will make their victory inevitable. The spies agree that they will rescue Rahab and her family when Jericho is conquered, provided that she continues to protect them. Rahab then uses a rope to let the spies down through a window in her house, which is built into the city wall so that leaving her house is also leaving the city itself.

When Joshua attacks Jericho, he orders that Rahab and her household alone be saved. He also sends the two spies back to her house to rescue her and her household. The story concludes with the comment that "her family has lived in Israel ever since. For she hid the messengers whom Joshua sent to spy out Jericho" (Josh 6:25).

Oddly enough, at least from the point of view of Matthew's genealogy, the Old Testament says nothing about a marriage of Rahab—either to Salmon or anyone else. Later Jewish tradition states that Rahab married Joshua, which is at least more believable than a marriage with Salmon, who would have lived some two centuries later! References to her in early Christian literature, as well as in Jewish tradition, confirm that she is highly regarded because of her heroic behavior on behalf of Israel (see Heb 11:31, Jas 2:25, *1 Clem.* 12:1).

The story of Ruth, the third woman in Matthew's genealogy, is better known than that of either Tamar or Rahab. A Moabite, Ruth becomes the daughter-in-law of Naomi, an Israelite who had migrated to Moab with her husband and sons to escape a famine. Following the death of Naomi's husband and sons, Naomi returns to Bethlehem, accompanied by Ruth. In order to secure food for herself and her mother-in-law, Ruth follows the harvesters to gather the barley that remains after the harvest. When Boaz, a relative of Naomi's, learns of Ruth's practice, he arranges for her to glean exclusively in his field because of her faithfulness to Naomi.

Upon learning of Boaz's kindness to Ruth, Naomi directs Ruth to go to Boaz at night and uncover the lower part of his body and wait for his instructions (Ruth 3:1–4). Ruth implores Boaz to "spread your cloak over your servant, for you are next-of-kin" (3:9). Boaz agrees to act as next-of-kin, that is, to marry Ruth, if no claim is made upon her by a closer male relative. Before daybreak, Boaz sends Ruth home with a generous supply of grain and immediately acts to secure Ruth as his wife. The witnesses respond to his action with the words: "We are witnesses. May the Lord make the woman who is coming into your house like Rachel and Leah, who together built up the house of Israel. May you produce children in Ephrathah and bestow a name in Bethlehem; and, through the children that the Lord will give you by this young woman, may your house be like the house of

Perez, whom Tamar bore to Judah" (4:11–12). The story concludes with the narrator's comment that Boaz and Ruth became the parents of Obed, who was the father of Jesse, who was in turn the father of David.

While there are several ambiguities in the narrative, it does hint at a sexual relationship between Ruth and Boaz during her visit to him at the threshing floor.[8] However, the response of the witnesses in 4:11–12 makes it clear that Ruth emerges from the narrative as a hero rather than as a woman accused of acting as a harlot. If subsequent Jewish tradition struggles with the figure of Ruth, it is because she, a Gentile, is the great-grandmother of King David, never because she is suspected of sexual immorality.

The fourth woman in Matthew's genealogy is "the wife of Uriah," and even that way of identifying her indicates that sexual immorality does play a role in the conception of Solomon. The story itself, found in 2 Samuel 11, begins when David, from the vantage point of the roof of his house, sees a beautiful woman in the midst of her bath. Although David's inquiry reveals that she is Bathsheba, the wife of Uriah, this information has little apparent effect on David, for the story continues: "So David sent messengers to get her, and she came to him, and he lay with her" (2 Sam 11:4). After her return home and the appropriate elapse of time, Bathsheba sends word to David that she is pregnant.

To avoid scandal, David calls for Uriah, who is engaged in battle with the Ammonites on David's behalf, and orders Uriah to return to his house. The assumption, of course, is that Uriah will have intercourse with his wife, and her pregnancy will thus escape notice. Uriah refuses the comforts of home and thereby spoils the plan, insisting that he cannot go home while David's other servants sleep in the field, campaigning against the Ammonites. When a second attempt to send Uriah home meets with the same results, David instructs his henchman Joab to place Uriah at the front of the battle, where he is killed. The episode concludes with the narrator's comment: "When the wife of Uriah heard that her husband was dead, she made lamentation for him. When the mourning was over, David sent and brought her to his house, and she became his wife, and bore him a son. But the thing that David had done displeased the Lord" (2 Sam 11:26–27). If the story leaves unclear the extent of the complicity of "the wife of Uriah" in her affair with David, the narrator's final comment assigns responsibility entirely to David. It is with David that God is displeased. The child conceived in adultery dies as a result of God's punishment (2 Sam 12:15b–23), but a second child, Solomon, is born to Bathsheba and David (2 Sam 12:24–25). Bathsheba's remaining appearances in 2 Samuel and 1 Kings concern her intervention on behalf of her son Solomon (1 Kgs 1:11–31) and eventually her unsuccessful intervention with King Solomon on behalf of Adonijah (1 Kgs 2:13–25).

Even this brief review of the stories of these women reinforces our initial impression that their appearance in Matthew's genealogy is, to say the very least, unusual. That fact has prompted a large number of explanations, out of which four general approaches dominate.

1. As early as the fourth-century church father Jerome, the four women are understood to be sinners. Tamar played the role of a harlot, and Rahab actually was a harlot. Ruth seduced Boaz, and Uriah's wife committed adultery. According to this theory, Matthew introduces these sinful women in order to show how Jesus comes to save people from their sins (cf. Matt 1:21) or perhaps in order to defend Mary against Jewish accusations. That is, there are sinful women in the acknowledged line of David so that slander against Mary has good precedent.

It is far from clear how the presence of these women furthers either the theological or the apologetic goal suggested. To insist that there are already sinful women in the Davidic line in no way defends Mary against the charge of sinfulness. Had Matthew merely wished to assert Jesus' role in saving people from their sins, the presence of sinful *men* in the genealogy would surely have sufficed (e.g., Judah, David, and Solomon)! Even the claim that the four women are sinners fails (except in the general sense in which all people may be said to be sinners), since Gen 38:26 proclaims Tamar's righteousness, Rahab emerges in later Jewish tradition as a model proselyte, and the narrator attaches neither scandal nor blame to Ruth. Although David and Bathsheba certainly enter into an adulterous relationship, we have seen that it is David whom the narrator identifies as the sinner—not Bathsheba.

2. A second approach, the one taken by the sixteenth-century reformer Martin Luther, locates the importance of the women in the fact that all of them are Gentiles. The biblical narratives refer to Tamar, Rahab, and Ruth as non-Israelites, and Matthew's identification of Bathsheba as "the wife of Uriah" focuses on the fact that he was a Hittite. The inclusion of Gentiles in the genealogy thus anticipates the role of Jesus as savior of Gentiles as well as of Jews. A major difficulty for this theory is that Mary, who is usually thought to be identified with the four other women in the genealogy, is a Jew, not a Gentile. Also, Matthew does not identify Uriah as a Hittite, making it uncertain that Matthew understands either Uriah or his wife to be a Gentile. While Tamar, Rahab, and Ruth are not Israelites, later Jewish tradition speaks of them as proselytes rather than as Gentiles.

3. A more recent approach, building on the notion that Matthew 1–2 seeks to counter Jewish claims about the origins of Jesus, argues that the four women are all points of controversy in Jewish discussion about whether the Messiah would come from the Davidic line. Those who argued against the Davidic messiahship pointed to these women as tainting the purity of the Davidic line, and those who argued for a Davidic Messiah were forced to

concede the place of these women (except for Rahab) in the ancestry of David and to interpret their presence as charitably as possible. Thus, Matthew includes the women because of tradition, and their presence reveals his insistence on the Davidic expectation.[9] As already noted, however, this approach is unable to account for the presence of Rahab, who is nowhere else understood to be part of the Davidic ancestry. More important, the approach relies heavily on Jewish texts that were written significantly later than the New Testament.[10]

4. Perhaps the most influential approach at present is that which finds the four women to have in common both extraordinary or irregular sexual unions which appeared to be scandalous and the fact that they took some initiative in their situations and were part of God's plan for the coming of the Messiah.[11] Matthew selects these women because they anticipate the role of Mary, whose pregnancy also has about it the taint of scandal and who is nevertheless part of God's plan. This approach has the advantage of offering a plausible connection between Mary and the other women in the genealogy, but once again it does not entirely fit the evidence. The category of "extraordinary or irregular unions" accounts well for Tamar and the "wife of Uriah," but it is difficult to say how Rahab's union with Salmon was extraordinary (leaving aside for the moment the historical problem of Salmon's having lived some two hundred years after Rahab). Ruth's *marriage* to Boaz, as distinct from any sexual relationship between the two prior to their marriage, is completely within the expectations of the levirate marriage code; indeed, that code prompts Naomi to send Ruth to Boaz in the first place (Ruth 3:1–4).

What all of these approaches have in common is the assumption that the four women (and, in some instances, Mary as well) must fit into a single category. They are all said to be sinners or Gentiles or blots on the Davidic messiahship or part of a scandalous union. Our brief review of their stories shows how much the women differ from one another and should raise questions about attempts to reduce these four distinct characters into one character.

At most, what the four women, or their stories, share is a common dynamic. None of them fits in with the way things are "supposed" to be. Each of the women is presented as threatening the status quo in some way, and each is in turn threatened. Each also is shown to be part of the divine plan, but that goes without saying since each appears in the genealogy because of the Davidic line.[12] The dynamic of threatening and being threatened dominates the entire story of Tamar and Judah, for Tamar's problem arises because Judah (wrongly) understands her to be a threat to the life of his only remaining son. Judah's injustice to her places Tamar in a threatened state, with neither husband nor child, and she seeks rectification through deception which again places her in a threatened state. Rahab poses a threat, not because she is a harlot or because her marriage is irregular, but because her knowledge of Joshua's spies jeopardizes the conquest. When Jericho eventually falls, Rahab in turn becomes the threatened one who must be delivered from the destruction of the remainder of the population. Ruth threatens the status quo by her decision (in contrast to Orpah's) to stay with Naomi and again by taking the initiative with Boaz. Her actions in both instances become dangerous for herself, since her alliance with Naomi could lead to starvation for them both and her advances to Boaz could lead to the charge of harlotry if he declines to fulfill his obligations as her kinsman. The one action attributed to the "wife of Uriah," the sending of the message of her pregnancy to David, threatens both David and Uriah (whom it eventually destroys); she subsequently becomes the one who lives under the threat of having no father for the child she carries.

The differing stories of Tamar, Rahab, Ruth, and the wife of Uriah do not, because of this shared dynamic, become one story. Each woman, of course, figures in the single "story" of the Davidic line. Each in her own way threatens that line and is in turn threatened. Each is delivered and the line preserved, although the circumstances of the women vary greatly.

When Mary's name appears in Matt 1:16, the final interruption of the customary form of "father begat son," we do not yet know the story or the threat that will play a role in it. Only in verses 18–25 does the threat posed by and to Mary emerge. The appearance of her name in verse 16, however, hints that such a threat surrounds her also. The wording of verse 16 differs both from the customary form and from the form used when the other women are introduced:

> Abraham begat Isaac
> Boaz begat Obed from Ruth
> Jacob begat Joseph the husband of Mary, from whom was begotten
>   Jesus the one called Christ.
>
> (author's translation)

Instead of either the expected "Joseph begat Jesus," or "Joseph begat Jesus from Mary," Joseph is identified as Mary's husband, and Mary as the woman who gave birth to Jesus. Matthew carefully avoids implying that Joseph was the biological father of Jesus, although the genealogy traces Jesus through the Davidic line because he is regarded legally as Joseph's son by virtue of Joseph's marriage to Mary and his naming of her child.[13] Verse 16, then, plays a complicated role in relationship to the rest of the genealogy and, indeed, in relationship to the rest of Matthew 1–2. On the one hand, it connects Joseph to Jesus as his legal father; on the other, it denies Joseph's biological paternity by declining to say that Mary's husband is also the one who begat Jesus.

Beyond this careful and even confusing distinction, verse 16 also introduces Mary and identifies her in two ways that become important in Matthew 2. Mary is Joseph's wife. The scene that makes this marriage a fact (1:18–25) will only confirm what the reader has already learned in 1:16. Mary is also the one through whom Jesus is born. The exact nature of the conception remains to be explained, but in its context 1:16 causes the reader to anticipate something out of the ordinary. Matt 1:17 brings the genealogy to a close by identifying three periods within the Davidic line and the number of generations in each period.[14]

The Birth of Jesus

As noted earlier in the discussion of the structure of Matthew 1–2, the entire first chapter fits together very closely. The scene in 1:18–25 constitutes not a second beginning for the Gospel but an amplification of the genealogy of 1:1–17. Here Matthew gives the explanation for his unusual manner of presenting Jesus' birth in verse 16. Verse 18a, then, resumes the reference to Jesus' origin in 1:1.

With the second part of this verse, the narrator tightly compresses crucial information:

> While his mother Mary was engaged to Joseph, but before they
> had come together she was found to be pregnant of the Holy
> Spirit.
>
> (author's translation)

Here again, as in verse 16, Mary's identification consists of her relationship to Jesus ("his mother") and to Joseph. Even the fact that Mary is not yet Jesus' mother does not prevent Matthew from identifying her as such.

Mary's relationship with Joseph reflects the social practice of early Judaism, in which a marriage took place in two stages. In the first stage, a man and woman agreed to the marriage in the presence of witnesses and were thereafter legally regarded as married to one another. During this period, sexual intercourse between the two was forbidden. In the second stage, the man took the woman to live in his home. Even in the first stage, however, the man had legal rights concerning his wife, so that any sexual involvement by her with another man was regarded as adultery.

When Matthew describes Mary and Joseph as engaged but not yet living together, then, nothing out of the ordinary has entered the story. It is only with the words "she was found to be pregnant" that the unusual occurs. Since sexual intercourse between Mary and Joseph was forbidden, her pregnancy violates the expected chain of events and threatens her very well-being. The dynamic of threat posed by and to a woman and to the Davidic line again enters the story.

It is futile to ask who finds that Mary is pregnant and what circumstances accompany that discovery. Similarly, we are not to imagine that someone instantly concluded that Mary's pregnancy was "of the Holy Spirit" or that such news was conveyed to Joseph. Verse 18b sets the stage for what is to follow. It has more in common with a narrator's direct address to an audience when he or she is introducing a scene than it does with a dramatic scene itself. The audience is assured that Mary's pregnancy is without scandal, although Joseph is not privy to this crucial information.

The final words of this verse, "of the Holy Spirit," will be repeated by the angel in verse 20. Unlike Gabriel's annunciation to Mary in Luke, nothing is said here of Mary's having found favor with God (Luke 1:30). Nor does Matthew satisfy modern curiosity regarding the way in which the Holy Spirit is responsible for the conception of Jesus. The point, instead, is that the Holy Spirit *is* responsible for Jesus' conception.

Having introduced the threat of Mary's pregnancy, the scene now opens upon Joseph as he prepares to respond. Joseph, her husband, is "a righteous man and unwilling to expose her to public disgrace" (1:19). The description of Joseph as Mary's husband reiterates the connection between the two (1:16, 18) and indicates his legal rights regarding Mary. Among those rights is the right of divorce, even accompanied by a public trial in the case of adultery. Despite these rights, Matthew portrays Joseph as a man who wishes to deal generously with Mary. A righteous person with no desire to make her shame a matter of public knowledge, Joseph resolves to "dismiss her quietly" (1:19). That is, he will divorce her.[15]

While there are various attempts to reconstruct historically the options available to Joseph, none of them explains how a genuinely secret or private divorce might be possible. Whatever action Joseph takes, Mary's pregnancy will scarcely remain a secret. Joseph's response to that pregnancy has now become a threat to Mary and to her baby. Whether legally charged with adultery or not, she may be forced to give birth to a child in scandal.

Joseph's decision to divorce Mary privately also anticipates the later action of Herod, who calls the magi to him in private (2:7). The contrasts between the righteous Joseph and Herod are striking, but the two men share a perception that Mary and Jesus constitute a threat, and both act in secret to address that threat.[16]

While Joseph is still considering his plan, an angel appears to him in a dream and instructs him concerning both Mary's pregnancy and the action he is to take. Joseph is not to be afraid to claim Mary as his wife, for her child is of the Holy Spirit. Joseph is to name the child Jesus. The angel explains that this event fulfills the prophetic word of Isa 7:14. Following the dream, Joseph does as he is ordered. The scene closes with the brief note that Mary gives birth to a son and Joseph names him Jesus.[17]

Joseph's first dream plays an important role in Matthew's Gospel by virtue of its claims that Jesus is conceived of the Holy Spirit, that he will save his people, that his birth fulfills prophecy. Along with these functions, the dream also leads Joseph to complete his marriage to Mary, thus removing from her and her child the threat of scandal or even death.[18]

The Threat of Herod

As we have already seen, part 2 of Matthew's narrative concerning Jesus' origin focuses on the geographical origin and destination of Jesus (Whence? Whither?), again employing the device of scriptural quotations that are being fulfilled in Jesus' life. The impetus for Jesus' geographical movements (to Egypt, from Egypt, to Nazareth) comes from the action of Herod, who is intent on destroying the young child whom Herod perceives as a threat to his own power. Throughout Matthew 2 there are parallels both to the biblical account of Moses' life and to developing Jewish tradition.[19]

Mary almost fades from our view in this part of Matthew's narrative. No longer the person who threatens the status quo, she is identified solely in connection with the infant Jesus. Although part 1 also identifies her as Jesus' mother and Joseph's wife, there the story focuses on the question of whether Joseph will divorce her, the angel's instruction that Joseph marry her, and her giving birth to Jesus. Although she speaks not a single word and is the subject of an active verb only as she gives birth (Matt 1:21, 25), she remains constantly in view.

In Matthew 2 the focus changes dramatically. Every reference to her in this story connects her with her child and makes her secondary to him:

On entering the house, they saw the child with Mary his mother. . . . (v. 11)

"Get up, take the child and his mother. . . ." (v. 13)

Then Joseph got up, took the child and his mother. . . . (v. 14)

"Get up, take the child and his mother. . . ." (v. 20)

Then Joseph got up, took the child and his mother. . . . (v. 21)

Apart from the visit of the magi, references to Mary appear only when Joseph is instructed to flee from Herod and to return from Egypt. The negative conclusion we might draw from this silence regarding Mary is that Matthew regards her as unimportant. She utters not a single word and takes not a single action. The actions for which she is the object are limited to being seen and being moved about.

The persistent use of the phrase "the child and his mother," however, should give us pause. While it is true that Matthew 2 refers to Mary only in connection with Jesus, it is also true that reference to Jesus almost always involves reference to Mary. With his consistent use of the phrase "the child and his mother" Matthew reflects a powerful connection between the two. When the magi finally arrive at the place of the star, they see both the child and Mary. The flight to Egypt involves not two parents and the child they protect but Joseph who is instructed to protect "the child and his mother." If Jesus is threatened, so is his mother. In Matthew's story, the two belong together.

By contrast with this silent Mary who is almost removed from view in Matthew 2, commentators often draw attention to the focalization of Matthew 2—indeed, of the entirety of Matthew 1 and 2—on Joseph. The genealogy of Joseph, his description as a good man, the three angelic visitations, the repeated use of his name—all these features distinguish Matthew's treatment of Joseph from his treatment of Mary. Especially when the Matthean narrative is compared with Luke 1–2, in which Joseph scarcely makes an appearance and the narrator gives considerable attention to Mary, the importance of Joseph in Matthew's opening chapters seems obvious.

This picture, however, somewhat exaggerates the role of Joseph in Matthew's Gospel. In the first place, the focalization on Joseph simply reflects the attention given father figures in a patriarchal society. More important, although it is true that Joseph is present as events unfold, he takes no part either in shaping events or in interpreting them. Even before Joseph comes on stage, the reader knows from the narrator's comments that he is or will be Mary's husband and that her pregnancy is of the Holy Spirit (1:16, 18). Only in his plan for dealing with Mary's pregnancy does he betray the smallest initiative (an initiative that threatens both Mary and the Messiah), and the angel's visitation quickly thwarts his decision. From that point on, Joseph's "actions" consist entirely of following the angel's instructions.

The only human being who takes significant, independent initiative in Matthew 1–2, amazingly enough, is Herod, the obvious villain of the piece. Herod seeks information about the promised Messiah, he contrives to have the magi bring him word about the infant Jesus, he orders all the infants of Bethlehem killed rather than risk being overthrown by this new "king." If Mary is passive and Joseph is first indecisive and then cooperative, Herod busily summons his troops. Neither Joseph nor Mary nor any other character emerges from Matthew 1–2 as fully developed as does Herod, a point that suggests that activity and attention do not alone reveal an author's assessment of a character.

Throughout his narrative of the origins of Jesus, Matthew is concerned to identify Jesus and especially to demonstrate how Scripture confirms that identity. Among the points Matthew underscores is that Jesus is already, even before his birth, threatened by those who do not understand him properly and whose own power is threatened by Jesus. The treatment of Mary in this narrative depicts her as posing a threat to Joseph and as being threatened in return.

MARY IN THE MINISTRY OF JESUS
(MATTHEW 12:46–50, 13:53–58)

Only twice does Matthew refer to Mary after the narrative of Jesus' origins in chapters 1 and 2. In 12:46–50, which parallels Mark 3:31–35 and Luke 8:19–21, Matthew tells of an incident in which Jesus' mother and brothers attempt to speak with him. And in 13:53–58, Jesus' countrymen make reference to Mary and other members of Jesus' family as they consider Jesus' identity and the source of his wisdom and power.

Matthew 12:46–50

Matthew's account of the visit of Jesus' mother and brothers, in common with its parallel in Luke, appears somewhat gentler than the harsh picture created by Mark's placement of this scene immediately after one in which friends of Jesus seek to take him home because they fear that Jesus may be mad (Mark 3:20–30). In Matthew, Jesus' mother and brothers come to the place where he has been teaching and ask to speak with him. He responds: "Who is my mother, and who are my brothers?" He then points to his disciples and says, "Here are my mother and my brothers! For whoever does the will of my Father in heaven is my brother and sister and mother" (12:48–50). Our first inclination is to ask whether this incident reveals a "positive" or a "negative" assessment of Mary and Jesus' brothers. The fact that they have come to speak with him might be taken to indicate that they wish to be associated with him, although this incident concludes a series of controversy stories in which Jesus is approached by those who are plainly hostile to him (12:1–8, 9–14, 22–32). Jesus' response, which does not acknowledge their relationship to him or even invite them to come inside, may reflect a negative assessment of Jesus' family.

The difficulties with all such reflection on this incident are of two sorts. First, the incident itself offers the occasion for Jesus to teach about discipleship, not about family relationships. The point here is that his disciples are to him as family, not that his family members are or are not part of that circle. The arrival of Jesus' mothers and brothers only provides opportunity for this teaching and has no material connection with the teaching itself.

Second, as we shall see, Luke's comments about Mary in the birth narrative draw attention to her response to and interpretation of events. By contrast, Matthew provides the reader with no clue whatsoever to Mary's understanding of Jesus and his role. We bring to the incident of the family's visit only the fact of their relationship. No previous knowledge influences our understanding of Mary and her assessment of Jesus. The incident itself tells us nothing new about Mary, apart from the reference to Jesus' brothers.[20]

Matthew 13:53–58

Matthew's remaining reference to Mary likewise adds little to our understanding of her and her role. In 13:53–58, Jesus teaches in the synagogue of "his own country," and the amazed neighbors respond: "Where did this man get this wisdom and these deeds of power? Is not this the carpenter's son? Is not his mother called Mary? And are not his brothers James and Joseph and Simon and Judas? And are not all his sisters with us? Where then did this man get all this?" (13:54–56).

Here Matthew includes names for the brothers of Jesus and mentions sisters as well. The elaborate listing of the members of Jesus' family dramatically illustrates the neighbors' point: Jesus cannot be the powerful and wise figure he pretends to be because his family is a known factor. Nothing particularly noteworthy about that family causes the neighbors to expect—or even accept—the possibility that they have produced a "prophet" (v. 57) or something more than a prophet. As was the case in 12:46–50, the incident focuses on varying responses to Jesus rather than on Mary or other members of Jesus' family.

CONCLUSION

At the beginning of this chapter I noted the temptation to read Matthew's initial narrative of Jesus' origins through the lens of Luke's birth narrative. That temptation becomes weighty indeed when we consider Matthew's characterization of Mary. As limited as are Mary's appearances in Luke-Acts, we shall see that she plays a variety of roles and serves to enhance the narrative tension of that work. Matthew's treatment of Mary is much more restricted. While there is tension regarding the threat to Mary and Jesus in Matthew 1–2, that tension is quickly resolved and does not persist into later chapters.

The Role of Mary

Mary's exclusive role in Matthew is that of mother. Matthew interprets that maternity, however, not in terms of an emotional attachment or anxiety or grief, but in terms of the possibilities for destruction that threaten Mary. Her juxtaposition with Tamar, Rahab, Ruth, and the wife of Uriah hints that she is vulnerable. In common with them, Mary's anomalous situation threatens those around her and, in turn, threatens her. Joseph may publicly repudiate her, jeopardizing her life and that of her child. Herod may succeed in finding and murdering the child—an act that would also destroy his mother (see 2:18). Mary is, throughout her appearances in Matthew 1 and 2, primarily an endangered figure. We learn nothing of her own thoughts, opinions, judgments, actions, desires; all we know of Mary is that she remains under threat of destruction.

Mary and Narrative Development

Mary's role in the developing narrative of Matthew is, to be sure, limited. Matthew's singular focus on the endangerment of Mary (and that of her child) anticipates the resistance to Jesus that runs throughout Matthew's Gospel. That resistance begins not even with Herod and his violent plot to kill the infant but with the good man Joseph, who contemplates an action that threatens Jesus along with Mary. Matthew does not explicitly refer back to these events surrounding Jesus' birth, but the emerging thread of resistance to Jesus should not be unexpected or unfamiliar to Matthew's readers.

Mary and the Order of Matthew

The governing principle or "order" of Matthew has to do with the fulfillment in Jesus Christ of God's history of salvation.[21] The salvation God brings about in Jesus Christ is also central to Luke-Acts, but Luke emphasizes the universal character of God's salvation, while Matthew emphasizes Jesus as the fulfillment of Scripture. Over and over again, Matthew interprets an event in Jesus' life with the formula "This took place to fulfill what had been spoken by the Lord through the prophet."

Mary's contribution to this governing principle is made quite explicit in the first formula quotation:

> Look, the virgin shall conceive and bear a son, and they shall name him Emmanuel. (1:23)

For Matthew, the most important function of Mary is to fulfill this prophecy.

Mary also figures in Matthew as the first to receive the salvation inaugurated in Jesus Christ, although this reception takes place in a way different from that in Luke. In Luke the calling of Mary is an act of grace, and she herself proclaims in it God's salvation to all (Luke 1:54–55). Matthew, by contrast, enacts Mary's salvation through the agency of the angel who intervenes to save her from Joseph's plan. Her salvation, like that of the women who precede her in Matthew's genealogy, depends on God's decision to use her in the fulfillment of his salvation of all people.

NOTES

1. Paul Minear, *Matthew: The Teacher's Gospel* (New York: Pilgrim Press, 1982). Following convention, I refer to the author of this Gospel as Matthew, without thereby assuming any particular identification of that individual.
2. "Quis et Unde?," in *Judentum, Urchristentum, Kirche: Festschrift für Joachim Jeremias,* ed. Walther Eltester (BZNW 26; Berlin: Alfred Töpelmann, 1960) 94–105. Stendahl also comments on the inappropriateness of calling Matthew 1–2 a birth narrative.
3. Raymond E. Brown, *The Birth of the Messiah* (updated edition; New York: Doubleday, 1993) 50–54.
4. While the term *genesis* also appears at the beginning of the depiction of Joseph's dream in 1:18–25, there it is resumptive of the *genesis* in 1:1 (see p. 40).
5. Stendahl, "Quis et Unde?," 100.
6. See the extensive discussion of the genealogy in Brown, *Birth,* 58–95, and the literature cited there.
7. See the discussion of the place of the Tamar story in its larger narrative context in Robert Alter, *The Art of Biblical Narrative* (New York: Basic Books, 1981) 5–12.
8. Such a possibility is discussed by Phyllis Trible, *God and the Rhetoric of Sexuality* (Philadelphia: Fortress, 1978) 182; E. F. Campbell, Jr., *Ruth* (AB7; Garden City, N.Y.: Doubleday, 1975) 131; C. M. Carmichael, "A Ceremonial Crux: Removing a Man's Sandal as a Female Gesture of Contempt," *JBL* 96 (1977) 332–33.
9. This explanation comes from Marshall Johnson, *The Purpose of the Biblical Genealogies with Special Reference to the Setting of the Genealogies of Jesus* (SNTSMS 8; Cambridge: Cambridge University Press, 1969) 139–210.

10. It also draws on a mistaken set of assumptions about Jewish messianic expectations. On this issue, see *Judaisms and Their Messiahs at the Turn of the Christian Era,* ed. Jacob Neusner, William S. Green, and Ernest Frerichs (Cambridge: Cambridge University Press, 1987).

11. See the discussion in Brown, *Birth,* 73–74, and in *Mary in the New Testament,* ed. Raymond E. Brown, Karl P. Donfried, Joseph A. Fitzmyer, and John Reumann (Philadelphia: Fortress, 1978) 81-83; Jane Schaberg's suggestion (see above, p. 9) is a variation on this thesis (*The Illegitimacy of Jesus: A Feminist Theological Interpretation of the Infancy Narratives* [San Francisco: Harper and Row, 1987] 32–35).

12. This suggestion amounts to an amplification of the fourth approach above, the major difference being that my suggestion does not identify the women's situations exclusively in terms of their marriages or sexual unions. This, in fact, is the difference between my approach and that of Schaberg.

13. On the historical circumstances that allow Joseph to be regarded as the legal father of Jesus, see the extensive discussion in Brown, *Birth,* 138–43.

14. On the difficulties in Matthew's enumeration of the generations, see Brown, *Birth,* 74–84.

15. Robert Brawley puts it rightly when he concludes that "there is nothing defective about Joseph's righteousness." Nevertheless, "the fallacy of good intentions is that Joseph is able to act out of the highest motivation but with insufficient knowledge so that he resolves to act against God's purposes rather than in conformity with them. The irony is that Joseph's good intentions remain intact as good intentions, nevertheless he works at shocking cross-purposes with God" ("Joseph in Matthew's Birth Narrative and the Irony of Good Intentions," *The Cumberland Seminarian* 28 [1990] 72).

16. It is possible that the adverb "quietly" (*lathra* in Greek) modifies "planned" rather than "dismiss." That way of translating the statement would resolve the need to explain the possibility of a secret or private divorce: Joseph is not planning a quiet divorce but making his plans in private, just as Herod does in 2:7.

17. Grammatically, it is possible that verse 25 says that Mary named him, since the verb may have either a male or female subject, but the command of the angel resolves any ambiguity.

18. In a highly suggestive essay on Matthew 1:18–25, Karl A. Plank describes the result of this passage as follows: "Mary, in her difference, brings to the world of Joseph the surprising presence of God. Remaining estranged from her, Joseph would stand alone in his purity, joined perhaps by moral peers but alienated from the God whose presence he would protect" ("The Human Face of Otherness," in *Faith and History: Essays in Honor of Paul W. Meyer,* ed. John T. Carroll, Charles H. Cosgrove, E. Elizabeth Johnson [Homage Series; Atlanta: Scholars, 1990] 73).

19. For a discussion of these parallels, see Brown, *Birth,* 112–16.

20. On the issue of Jesus having brothers, see the discussion of Luke 8:19–21, below, p. 70–71.

21. So Jack Dean Kingsbury, *Matthew as Story* (Philadelphia: Fortress, 1986) 134.

CHAPTER 3

Disciple, Prophet, and Mother

Mary in Luke-Acts

winged women was saying
"full of grace" and like.
was light beyond sun and words
of a name and a blessing.
winged women to only i.
i joined them, whispering
yes.

Lucille Clifton, "mary's dream"

As early as the opening lines of Luke's Gospel, readers perceive that they have entered a terrain markedly different from that created by Matthew. Whereas Matthew begins by identifying Jesus as "the son of David, the son of Abraham," thereby locating him firmly within the history of Israel, Luke begins with a formal preface such as would be found in the works of the historians of his day. Throughout Luke's two-volume work, consisting of the Gospel of Luke and the Acts of the Apostles, he presents what he terms "an orderly account" of the events that surrounded the formation of the early Christian community (Luke 1:3).[1]

By contrast with Matthew, Luke seems to give great attention to Mary, but stories that involve her actually occupy only a small portion of Luke's "orderly account." She plays a prominent role in the birth narrative (Luke 1:5–2:52), appears briefly in 8:19–21, and is referred to indirectly in 11:27–28. The sole remaining reference to Mary occurs in Acts 1:14, where Luke mentions her among those who gather in Jerusalem following the ascension of Jesus.

In common with other characters in Luke-Acts, Mary appears and disappears from the stage at Luke's direction and without explanation. For example, the opening chapter of Acts describes in considerable detail the selection of Matthias as a successor for Judas, prompting the reader to anticipate that Matthias will play some important role in the story that follows. He does not, however; in fact, he never again appears in the story. Even

Peter, who is undoubtedly a significant character in the first half of Acts, abruptly disappears following the Jerusalem council in Acts 15. The appropriate question about Mary, then, is not why we hear so little about her but what roles she plays and what those roles reveal about Luke's understanding of her.[2]

As we examine the various scenes in which Mary appears, in keeping with the earlier discussion of literary characterization, we shall attend especially to Mary's speech, her actions, descriptions of her by others (including the narrator), the ways in which she is juxtaposed with other characters, the progression of the story as it involves her, and her relationship to the overarching themes and concerns of Luke-Acts.

What we shall see differs dramatically from Matthew's treatment of Mary. Mary will assume three distinct but interrelated roles. At times Luke portrays her as one of the disciples, perhaps even as an exemplary disciple. In the birth narrative itself she wraps herself in the mantle of a prophet, one inspired by God to proclaim the hidden things God is accomplishing among the people. Finally, and by no means of least importance, Luke describes Mary simply as a mother. It is in connection with this role that she contributes an important element of tension to the beginning of Luke's narrative.

THE BIRTH NARRATIVE (LUKE 1:5–2:52)

An earlier generation of scholarship on Luke-Acts tended to read the birth narrative in isolation from the remainder of Luke-Acts. Hans Conzelmann's work on Luke's theology set the agenda for students of Luke in the second half of this century. He argued that the birth narratives were not an original component of Luke's Gospel and, for that reason, he virtually excluded Luke 1–2 from his consideration of Luke's theology.[3] Although subsequent critics have, in theory, rejected this dichotomy between the birth narrative and the remainder of Luke-Acts, the view that the birth narrative was composed later than the rest of the Gospel has resulted in a tendency to interpret it in isolation from the remainder of Luke's work.

Even those scholars who posit a close theological relationship between the birth narrative and the remainder of the Gospel typically understand some parts of the infancy narrative as late additions. Raymond Brown, for example, argues that 2:41–52, the story of the twelve-year-old Jesus in the Jerusalem temple, circulated independently and was added at a late stage in Luke's composition.[4] Such views result in what has been called an "archaeological" approach to the text, digging through historical layers to determine what traditions are earliest. Since this study is concerned primarily with literary rather than historical questions, I shall read through the text in its present form, reading with Luke's readers rather than with the process of Luke's composition.

When issues of history dominate the discussion, the fulcrum of discussion regarding Mary in Luke-Acts becomes the statement in 1:38, "Here I am, the servant of the Lord." That is because the final scene in the birth narrative, 2:41–52, is regarded as almost an intrusion that does not belong. If we are reading from beginning to end, however, the question becomes what it means that the story begins with the "servant of the Lord" and ends with Mary's question to Jesus in 2:48 and the narrator's concluding remarks about Mary's brooding and Jesus' growth.

The Annunciation and Mary's Consent

Following the preface in 1:1–4, Luke begins his account with the story of the annunciation to Zechariah concerning the birth of John the Baptist. As is the case throughout Luke 1–2, allusions to stories from the Old Testament are manifold and, indeed, the annunciation to Zechariah parallels the annunciations to Hagar, Abraham, and the mother of Samson. In common with their predecessors, Zechariah and Elizabeth have no reasonable expectation of offspring, the conception removes scandal from the barren mother, the child to be born will bring about deliverance for the people.

The annunciation to Mary in 1:26–38 parallels that to Zechariah as well as paralleling numerous features of birth annunciations in the Old Testament. Raymond Brown uses the colorful analogy of the diptych, a pair of paintings that stand together and interpret one another, to illustrate the way in which these two annunciations interpret one another.[5] Alongside the parallels between these stories, however, we shall find that the annunciation to Mary at virtually every point surpasses that to Zechariah. In numerous details Luke contrasts the birth of Jesus with that of John, even as the stories are structurally the same.

"In the sixth month the angel Gabriel was sent by God to a town in Galilee called Nazareth" (1:26). Even with these initial words, the narrator connects the two stories of Elizabeth and of Mary. The "sixth month" can only be the sixth month of Elizabeth's pregnancy, just referred to in the preceding verses; in verse 19 Gabriel identifies himself as the angel who speaks to Zechariah. But on this occasion Gabriel visits not a priest in the great temple in Jerusalem "in the days of King Herod of Judea." Instead, Gabriel goes to Galilee, to the city of Nazareth, in the time of Elizabeth's miraculous pregnancy. The irony of Jesus' birth begins here. He is born outside of the holy place and apart from the center of power, in God's time rather than in the time of King Herod.

Gabriel's second announcement takes him "to a virgin engaged to a man whose name was Joseph, of the house of David. The virgin's name was Mary" (1:27). Virtually all of the concrete information that we will learn about Mary appears in this lean description:

> to a virgin
> engaged to a man whose name was Joseph of the house of David.
> The virgin's name was Mary.

The contrast with the expansive description of Zechariah and Elizabeth is striking. There Luke explains that Zechariah is a priest, both he and Elizabeth are upright and blameless before God, both are old, they have no child (1:5–7).

Luke's first statement is that the person whom Gabriel visited was a *parthenos,* a virgin. To concentrate on the term *virgin* in a narrow biological sense is to miss the point here. While *parthenos* can designate one who has not engaged in sexual intercourse, it very often refers simply to a young woman.[6] That is surely how a reader unfamiliar with the story would take it *at this point,* especially given the contrast between the age and barrenness of Elizabeth and the youth and potential for fertility suggested by the identification *parthenos.* That Mary may eventually become a mother is suggested by the second feature of her description, "engaged to a man whose name was Joseph." We might expect to learn the name of Mary's father (see 2:36), but the only family ascribed to her is that of the man she will marry, Joseph. All we ever know of Joseph is that he is "of the house of David."[7]

"The virgin's name was Mary" not only gives us a crucial detail, the name, but also reiterates Mary's identity as *parthenos.* This story formally resembles the one that has just preceded it and numerous annunciations in the Old Testament, but this one word indicates that something very distinctive will happen here. Mary is not the aging Sarah or the barren Hannah, whose plea for a child will finally be answered. She does not fit the pattern of the elderly barren women of the Old Testament, and she makes no request of God for the gift of a child.

Instead, Mary finds herself addressed: "Greetings, favored one! The Lord is with you." The initial word of greeting is tantamount to the ordinary salutation "Hello" or "Good morning," but what follows shapes the story that lies ahead: "favored one! The Lord is with you." Here what must be regarded as a reliable character makes an announcement about Mary: she is favored with God; the Lord is with her.[8] In and of itself the announcement reveals little, but it does cause the reader to wonder what it is about Mary that makes her favored with God. The announcement also serves to introduce the statement that will follow in verses 30–33.

Mary's response underscores the tension that the announcement introduces into the story. The announcement frightens her and causes her to
consider what the greeting means (cf. Luke 1:12). Gabriel's response neatly
parallels the comment to Zechariah in verse 13:

Do not be afraid, Zechariah, for your prayer has been heard.

Do not be afraid, Mary, for you have found favor with God.

As was also the case with Zechariah, the injunction against fear is followed
by an announcement; the first part focuses on Mary and the second on the
one who is to be born.

"You have found favor with God." Gabriel's opening line of annunciation restates verse 28. Once again, no reason is given for Mary's having
found favor. Here Mary's story contrasts with that of Zechariah and Elizabeth, whose goodness the narrator takes care to elaborate (1:6; compare Acts
10:1–4). Instead of explaining how Mary has arrived at this standing, Gabriel announces its consequences: "And now [lit., behold!] you will
conceive in your womb and bear a son, and you will name him Jesus." The
remaining lines of the annunciation identify the child and his role, but this
initial line addresses Mary. The three verbs in the second person singular
describe the promise that is being made to her: "*you* will conceive . . .[and
you will] bear a son, and *you* will name him. . . ." The introductory formula, "And now," insists on the importance of what is to follow.

Small wonder that Mary's first spoken words concern her own situation:
"How can this be, since I am a virgin [lit., know no man]?" A variety of historical reconstructions have attached themselves to this ambiguous question.[9]
Whatever the intended meaning of the question, it accomplishes several things
in the narrative. While it parallels the question of Zechariah in 1:18, Mary is
(unlike Zechariah) not punished for her objection. The question recalls the initial statement that Mary is a *parthenos,* although here the emphasis does fall
on Mary's biological virginity. The question also has the important function
of allowing Gabriel to comment further on the birth that is to occur.

Gabriel's "answer" to Mary's question has three distinct parts. First, he
explains that the "how" of Jesus' birth has to do with God's action through
the Holy Spirit (v. 35). Second, he reveals Elizabeth's pregnancy to Mary.
This revelation serves as a sign guaranteeing that the annunciation to Mary
is also reliable. Third, Gabriel explains that "nothing will be impossible with
God." This final statement may be more important in the story as a whole
than is often recognized. Mary cannot have a baby, because she has "known
no man." But Gabriel's annunciation asserts that what *cannot* happen indeed
will happen. God is doing that which is impossible.

Once again the parallel with the story of Elizabeth and Zechariah serves to reinforce the uniqueness of Mary's situation. The pregnancy of Elizabeth is at least improbable, as the dumbfounded Zechariah acknowledges (1:18), but that pregnancy does have antecedents in the history of Israel. It is improbable, or even "impossible," just as are the pregnancies of Sarah and Rachel and Hannah. A reader with even the vaguest notions of Israel's history would recognize in the annunciation to Zechariah this familiar theme. While the annunciation to Mary parallels these stories at many points, it also contrasts with them. Mary, who is neither old nor barren nor well known for her goodness, will bear a child. If the other conceptions are to be thought of as something like miracles of healing, this one is virtually a miracle of creation.[10]

At this point in the narrative, the parallels with the annunciation to Zechariah might lead us to expect a narrator's note about the conception of Jesus (1:24; compare Gen 21:1–2; 1 Sam 1:20). Instead, this annunciation culminates in Mary's consent: "Behold, the slave of the Lord. Let it be with me according to your word" (author's translation). Once again the word "behold" draws attention to what follows. Mary claims for herself the title *hē doulē kyriou*. Although the NRSV translates *doulē* as "servant," there can be no doubt that what the word means is "slave."[11] Mary recognizes with this statement God's selection of her and the compulsion under which her role is to be played. To translate "servant" is to misconstrue Mary's role as that of one who has *chosen* to serve rather than one who has *been chosen*.

The difficulty with applying the title "slave of the Lord" to Mary arises because generations of Christians have seen Mary as a model or example for all women and have distorted her slavery to the Lord to mean the subjection of women in general to men in general. That misinterpretation of the text, however, does not give us license to make the text into what it is not. The title "slave of the Lord" indicates the authority of God in human salvation and says nothing about the authority of men and women in relation to one another. Quite to the contrary, if Mary is *God's* slave, then she cannot at the same time be the slave of human beings. Elsewhere in Luke-Acts, the term *slave* is used to refer to those who serve God and rightly understand God's authority in their lives (see, e.g., Acts 2:18, 4:29, 16:17). In his letters Paul speaks of himself as a slave (Rom 1:1; compare Rom 6:16–20; 1 Cor 7:21–23) and insists that he serves under compulsion (1 Cor 9:16). "Slave of the Lord," then, is a title that may well be applied to every believer.

The conclusion of verse 38 indicates that Mary consents to that service: "Let it be with me according to your word." Mary has not chosen this task for herself, any more than the apostles will later choose their own roles, but she does consent to it. Some traditional interpretations of Mary see in these words the emergence of Mary as a model for all women, but it is difficult to find anything in the text that suggests such an identification between Mary and women in general. With her words of compliance Mary becomes not a model female but a model disciple who consents to what is not yet fully understood.[12] This is a role Mary will play again in Luke-Acts, but, as the story will reveal, it is not her only role.

Mary and Elizabeth

Although the scene changes, Mary remains the focus of attention. Indeed, her actions set the stage for what follows. She "set out and went with haste . . . , she entered . . . and greeted." To this narrative transition Luke adds a few words that further intertwine the events of the two annunciations. Mary goes "with haste." It is not clear whether her haste derives from the urgent need to confirm Gabriel's sign or from the astonishing news of her own pregnancy. Whatever the cause, Mary's haste brings together Gabriel's words to her and her visit to Elizabeth. Her haste is recalled when the shepherds hasten to Bethlehem following the angelic announcement of Jesus' birth (2:16).

When Mary "enters" she enters "the house of Zechariah," recalling his plight and again contrasting his unwillingness to hear with Mary's willingness. He serves as a foil for Mary, emphasizing her obedience and his own continuing inability to speak. That inability on his part is also eloquently echoed by contrasts with both Elizabeth and Mary, who burst into glorious spirit-inspired speech.

Although it is Zechariah's house that she enters, Mary's greeting addresses Elizabeth and prompts Elizabeth's statement about Mary. This is now the second character who speaks concerning Mary, and we have no indication that either of them is to be regarded with suspicion. Because it comes from an angel, Gabriel's speech can hardly be questioned, and Elizabeth's likewise is trustworthy, for she herself is not only "righteous," but she also speaks by means of the Holy Spirit (v. 41).

Elizabeth's words of greeting to Mary underscore what Gabriel has announced earlier. Several specific statements of Elizabeth's repeat and reinforce the annunciation.

Elizabeth	Gabriel
Blessed are you among women	You have found favor with God
Blessed is the fruit of your womb	You will conceive . . .
The mother of my Lord	Son of the Most High
The child in my womb leaped for joy	The Holy Spirit will come upon you
Blessed is she who believed	Here am I, the servant of the Lord

Although Elizabeth's outcry contains no new information about Mary, it reinforces the portrait already emerging by displaying it from the quite different perspective of Elizabeth.

Each of Elizabeth's statements addresses Mary as a woman and, especially, as one whose maternity is itself a sign of God's blessing. In the place of Gabriel's assertion "You have found favor with God," Elizabeth cries, "Blessed are you among women." With the phrases "the fruit of your womb," "the mother of my Lord," and "the child in my womb leaped for joy," Elizabeth's words draw attention to the reality of both pregnancies and the joy that accompanies them. While Gabriel's statements both to Zechariah and to Mary focus on the future greatness of John and Jesus respectively, Elizabeth's cry attests that the Spirit is breaking in even in the present.

Elizabeth's closing words praise Mary for her confidence in the promise that has been made to her. Taken together with Mary's consent to the words of Gabriel, these closing words offer our only insight into why Mary may be said to have "found favor" with God. Or better, since the declaration of Mary's favor with God precedes her act of consent, these words characterize Mary's *response* to the favor bestowed upon her.

The Magnificat, which comes as Mary's response to the greeting of Elizabeth, begins with the abrupt introduction, "And Mary said."[13] The speech itself is virtually a pastiche of texts taken from the Old Testament. The story of Hannah and her song at the birth of Samuel strongly influence the Magnificat, although many other biblical texts echo in Mary's words.[14] And yet, in the Lukan context, it is Mary who gives voice to these words. Her situation interprets the Magnificat, and the Magnificat in turn reveals something of who Luke understands her to be. To examine the Magnificat only as a collection of quotations from Scripture or only as evidence of a pre-Lukan source is to overlook the significant question of what purpose it has in the present context. Whatever the history or source of the Magnificat, here it serves as *Mary's* interpretation of the events taking place, and the question for this study is what it reveals about her.

In the words of praise that introduce the Magnificat ("My soul magnifies the Lord, and my spirit rejoices in God my savior"), Mary's haste to reach Elizabeth takes shape in words. No longer merely submissive to Gabriel's annunciation, she offers thanksgiving to God who is both Lord and savior. In these lines and those that follow, any notion that Mary has earned her selection seems banished by her emphasis on God's gift to her. As Raymond Brown notes, Elizabeth's canticle praises Mary, but Mary's praises God.[15]

The first section of the Magnificat (vv. 48–50) gives reasons for the praise of God, beginning with God's regard for "the low estate of his slave" (author's translation). Because this statement echoes those of Hannah and Leah (1 Sam 1:11, Gen 29:32), commentators sometimes puzzle over the fact that Mary is not barren as were her predecessors. This too-literal reading overlooks the connection between the *doulē* of the Magnificat and Mary's claim of that title for herself in 1:38. Her "lowliness" may take a different form than that of Hannah and Leah, but Mary is, no less than they, to be identified with the poor and the powerless, as the rest of the Magnificat, and indeed the rest of the birth narrative, will demonstrate. The form of Mary's "lowliness" is here announced and will be explained in the lines that follow.

The blessing that all generations will bestow on Mary "magnifies" or extends the blessing already bestowed on her through the agency of Gabriel and the greeting of Elizabeth. What is new here is not the blessing of Mary but its extent: "all generations" will regard her as blessed *because* of the One who has blessed her. Again, Mary's blessedness derives from God's gift rather than from some inherent goodness of her own. This proclamation in verse 48b begins with "Surely" (lit., "And behold"), insisting yet again on the surprising nature of God's intervention.

In verses 51–52, Mary connects God's action in her own case with the prophetic motif of God's overturning things as they are: God has "scattered the proud" and "brought down the powerful." The movement from God's blessing of Mary to God's action for all people is not arbitrary but interprets God's action in Mary's case as part of a larger history of God's acts of salvation. This passage (vv. 50–53) anticipates the scene in Nazareth when Jesus announces that the prophecy of good news is being fulfilled (Luke 4:16–30); it is not Jesus who introduces that motif in the Gospel of Luke, but Mary, who sees in herself a specific instance of God's salvation of the poor and the humble.

The closing lines of the Magnificat (vv. 54–55) place it firmly within the context of God's covenant faithfulness with Israel. Luke presents Mary's conception as a miraculous event, tantamount to a new creation, and Mary interprets that event as part of a larger pattern of God's overturning the things that are, but those claims have meaning only within the history of God's actions for Israel. All that occurs does so "in remembrance of his mercy, according to the promise he made to our ancestors, to Abraham and to his descendants for ever." Mary's speech, then, connects her own situation as the lowly slave of God to that of Israel ("to Abraham and to his descendants forever"). Indeed, the connection forged here between Mary and Israel is sufficiently close that some commentators speak of her as the "representative" or even the "personification" of Israel.[16] Such language perhaps overstates the matter, but it does forcefully draw attention to the way in which the Magnificat depicts Mary speaking with and for Israel.

The scene closes with the narrator's comment that Mary stayed with Elizabeth for three months, continuing the web of connections Luke makes between the two women and their pregnancies. The additional comment that Mary "returned to her home" continues the pattern in this narrative of having scenes close with departures (cf. 1:23, 38; 2:20, 39). It also carefully and perhaps even deliberately avoids identifying Mary with anyone else's home. She has not yet gone to live with Joseph, and indeed only his name has appeared so far in Luke's story and that only once (1:27). We might have anticipated that Mary would return to the home of her father, but no such reference appears. Whatever connections or identifications belong to Mary, for Luke she has importance exclusively as the "favored one." Given the way in which Mary has been viewed as the exemplary female, this singular identification might lead to the conclusion that women are significant only as they are mothers or wives as Mary was to be mother of Jesus and wife of Joseph. Notice, however, that Luke often "reduces" people to singular features; for example, he introduces Saul as the church's enemy (Acts 9:1–5); Peter is the spokesperson for the community (Acts 2:14–36). That does not mean that these people as historical figures had only one dimension, but that the narrator has chosen, out of all the stories to be told, a particular feature to enhance as part of the overall design of the narrative.

In the Magnificat, in fact, Mary's role changes from her role in the annunciation-and-consent scene. In that scene, Mary hears of her son's birth, and she consents to her role as "slave of the Lord." Perhaps more than any other scene in the Lukan birth narrative, at the annunciation Mary clearly functions as a disciple, one who "follows" (cf. 5:27–28). During her visit to Elizabeth, however, Mary moves from being the object of Elizabeth's praise to becoming the interpreter of the gospel.

Mary's role in this scene warrants identifying her as a prophet, a role that bears great significance in the Lukan story.[17] Luke does not identify her by that title, however, which may seem puzzling. He does explicitly claim that both Elizabeth (1:41) and Zechariah (1:67) speak by means of the Holy Spirit, which makes his silence regarding Mary's speech in the Magnificat all the more curious. On the other hand, Gabriel's announcement that "the Holy Spirit will come upon you" (1:35) may suggest that the Spirit is responsible not only for Mary's pregnancy but also for her speech. In addition, Luke may refrain from identifying Mary's speech as prophetic since she will appear among those who experience the outpouring of the Spirit on the day of Pentecost (see Acts 1:14, 2:1–4); that is, while Mary functions prophetically in the Magnificat, Luke reserves the reference to the Spirit for its decisive appearance at Pentecost.[18]

One more feature of the narration requires our attention. In both annunciation accounts, Gabriel's words about John and Jesus are couched in the future tense. Given that these annunciations concern the future births of the two babies, there is nothing remarkable in that fact. Neither Elizabeth nor

Mary, however, speaks in the future tense. Elizabeth's outcry is one that praises Mary and her (future) offspring in the present. Stranger yet, Mary's words announce what God has *already* done, as if the gospel itself were an accomplished fact. This alteration reflects Luke's view that Jesus' conception and birth are, in themselves, salvific (see Simeon's words in 2:29–32). But the alteration also has the effect of bringing the promised event into the present. No longer is the promise, like its predecessor, the promise to Abraham and Sarah, one that will be fulfilled at some time in the future. With the joyous exchange of Elizabeth and Mary, the fulfillment of the promise already begins.

The Birth of Jesus

Following Mary's return home, Luke narrates the birth of John and his subsequent circumcision and naming. These events take place without a single reference to Mary or the impending birth of Jesus, but the parallel between the two annunciations leads the reader to anticipate the birth of Jesus, and the significance ascribed to John's birth (both through the overcoming of Elizabeth's barrenness and through Zechariah's canticle) points toward the fulfillment of Mary's prophecy in the Magnificat.

Whereas the story in 1:57–80 focuses on John and his birth and importance, the scene that opens in 2:1 masterfully understates the importance of Jesus' birth. As in every previous scene in the birth narrative, Luke begins the story of Jesus' birth with a reference to time (cf. 1:5, 26, 39, 57). Here, however, time is not counted in terms of Elizabeth's pregnancy or in terms even of the reign of Herod, but in terms of the Roman empire. The opening reference to the time of Caesar Augustus and his decree threatens to overshadow everything else in the story.

Reinforcing this virtual eclipse of Mary's pregnancy is the order in which characters appear in the opening lines. The weighty introductions of the person of Caesar Augustus, followed by the local ruler Quirinius, "all" who go to be enrolled in the census, and the singular figure of Joseph, cause us to lose track of the anticipated parallel to John's birth. Indeed, the promise to Israel itself seems lost on this world stage. Only when the narrator has reached the end of the explanation of Joseph's trip to Bethlehem do we learn that Mary was along with him.

With the birth itself in verses 6–7, the narrator abruptly focuses on Mary:

> And while they were there the days of her pregnancy (lit., her giving birth) were fulfilled

and she gave birth to her firstborn son
and she swaddled him
and she lay him in a manger because there was no place for
them in lodging.

(author's translation)

Apart from the introductory notice regarding the time of Mary's delivery, and the closing notice about place, three active verbs describe the events, each of which has Mary as its subject and the babe as its object. Here Mary acts alone. No word of bystanders interprets this event. Even Joseph remains hidden from the narrator's vision.

It is customary to note how little detail Luke gives to the birth of Jesus. Despite the fact that it has been anticipated since Gabriel's visit, the birth itself takes place with scant comment from the narrator. In fact, it appears to be an utterly ordinary event in the shadow of the reign of Caesar Augustus and his decision to carry out a census of the whole world. Historical questions about the census need not prevent our understanding that it conveys the vast power of this world ruler. Whether Luke wants to suggest that the infant born to Mary will eventually subvert the reign of Caesar Augustus and his successors is unclear. What is clear is the irony that emerges when the seemingly ordinary, insignificant Mary gives birth to her seemingly ordinary, insignificant baby within the confines of Caesar's attempt at control through counting (i.e., the census).

What Luke writes about Jesus' birth is almost a notice rather than a description; nevertheless, what we have in 2:7 expands on the usual birth notice in biblical narratives. In Luke 1:57, we read simply that the time for Elizabeth to give birth was fulfilled and she bore a son (cf. Matt 1:25). Similarly, the stories in the Old Testament from which Luke draws throughout the birth narrative contain only the briefest notices about the actual births:

> Hagar bore Abram a son; and Abram named his son, whom Hagar bore, Ishmael. (Gen 16:15)

> Sarah conceived and bore Abraham a son in his old age, at the time of which God had spoken to him. (Gen 21:2)

> In due time Hannah conceived and bore a son. . . . (1 Sam 1:20)

Comparison with these earlier stories reveals not only that Luke's account expands on these birth notices but also that there are two simple narrative expansions here that prove to be important. In addition to the customary statement that Mary gave birth, Luke specifies that she wrapped the baby and that she placed him in a manger. Since both of these statements are repeated in the angelic proclamation in verse 12, and verse 16 repeats the reference to the manger, they may bear some particular role in the story. While controversy abounds regarding the historical connotations of each of these two details, in relation to one another they form an interesting contradiction. The wrapping of Jesus, in and of itself an utterly normal practice, hardly worthy of notice, nevertheless conveys the nurturing care associated with loving parenthood (compare Wis 7:4). This child has someone who will see to his needs. Placing him in a manger, an object otherwise used for the feeding of animals, signals that Mary and Jesus alike have no place. By creating this small conflict between Mary's appropriate care for Jesus (swaddling) and the insignificance of both of them (they have no place), Luke introduces a minor element of narrative tension concerning Jesus.[19]

Abruptly, the narrator shifts from Mary and her action with the newborn to the unlikely scene of angels who reveal the good news of this birth to a group of shepherds, directing them to go and see the child. Like Mary on her visit to Elizabeth, the shepherds go "with haste" to find "Mary and Joseph, and the child lying in the manger." The ordering of the characters found by the shepherds is puzzling, especially since their instructions make no mention of either Mary or Joseph. Perhaps again here Luke contrasts the presence of both parents with the absence of an appropriate place for the infant to lie.

The response to the shepherds' story again brings Mary to the foreground: "And all who heard marveled over what was said to them by the shepherds; and Mary kept all these things, considering them in her heart. And the shepherds went away glorifying and praising God for all they had heard and seen, just as had been told them" (2:17–20; author's translation). Mary's response to their visit stands between two other responses and contrasts sharply with them both. In the responses that surround that of Mary, there is at least the impression of verbal exchange, perhaps even loud exaltation or cries of amazement and confusion. Mary, however, remains silent. While "all who heard" marvel *at what the shepherds told them* and the shepherds rejoice *in what they heard and saw*, the cause of Mary's response is unclear (cf. also 1:66). The narrator does not explicitly connect Mary's "pondering" with the event of the shepherds; "all these things" undoubtedly includes their visit, but it may refer to earlier events as well. Perhaps most important, the narrator makes clear that those who surround Mary respond with amazement and awe, but the verbs that describe Mary's response connote neither wonder nor praise but perhaps secrecy or even isolation. Where earlier her own fear yielded to consent (1:38) and even praise (1:46–55), here her response stands uninterpreted.

Similar statements in the Old Testament underscore the impression of ambiguity here. When Joseph begins to dream of his future greatness, Jacob's response sets him apart from Joseph's brothers, but it is not clear what Jacob thought or feared about his troublesome son: "So his brothers were jealous of him [Joseph], but his father kept the matter in mind" (Gen 37:11).[20] Daniel concludes the narration of one of his dreams with the comment: "As for me, Daniel, my thoughts greatly terrified me, and my face turned pale; but I kept the matter in my mind" (Dan 7:28; see also Dan 7:15, 8:27; T. Levi 6:2).

These two stories do not form an easy parallel with Luke 2, but they may suggest that Mary's response is intended to be unclear. She understands some things, but much about her son and his future remains unclear and perhaps even troublesome. By means of this unclarity, Luke interjects a bit of narrative tension, both about who Jesus is and about where Mary's *pondering* will lead. This motif of not understanding begins with Zechariah, where it is part of the stereotypical response to the divine presence, and it continues in Mary's reaction to Gabriel, but it takes on a different texture in this passage and later at the end of chapter 2, where no reassurance or explanation resolves the tension.

Simeon and Anna

As Zechariah's prophecy follows the birth of John the Baptist, the prophecies of Simeon and Anna follow and further interpret the birth of Jesus. Luke sets the stage for these events by explaining that Mary and Joseph take Jesus to the temple in Jerusalem to present him to the Lord (vv. 22–24). Although the legal requirements being fulfilled are somewhat confused here,[21] the literary context is quite clear. Like Hannah with Samuel (1 Sam 1:24), Mary presents her infant in the holy place, establishing (along with the annunciation to Zechariah in 1:5–20) the importance of Jerusalem and its temple for the whole of the Lukan narrative.

The introduction of Simeon reports his credentials. In keeping with Luke's practice elsewhere (Zechariah, Cornelius, Ananias), he leaves no possibility for doubting the veracity or credibility of Simeon's words. Not only do we learn that Simeon is a righteous man who anticipates Israel's redemption and who has the gift of the Spirit, but both verses 26 and 27 specify the Spirit's activity upon him. We expect that, like Gabriel, Elizabeth, Mary, and the unnamed angel who addresses the shepherds, Simeon may be trusted.

Simeon speaks twice. In verses 29–32 he holds the infant Jesus and addresses God directly. Simeon praises God for the gift of witnessing God's salvation. In language that both recalls Isa 49:6 and will echo throughout Luke-Acts (e.g., Acts 26:17–18, 28:28), Simeon describes God's salvation as "a light for the revelation of the Gentiles and glory to thy people Israel." Even in its brevity Simeon's canticle epitomizes the themes about John and Jesus as they have emerged in the birth narratives. God has prepared salvation (2:31), just as John the Baptist will prepare the people for God (1:17, 76). The salvation inaugurated in the birth of Jesus means glory for Israel (2:32), in keeping with Mary's words about the promises to Israel (1:54–55; cf. 1:77). While Simeon's canticle expands the scope of God's salvation to include the Gentiles, the canticle otherwise contains nothing that is unexpected. By this point in the narrative, readers know that the births of John and of Jesus portend the salvation of the people. The parents of Jesus, here unnamed, respond with the astonishment that earlier characterizes pronouncements about Jesus' (or John's) future greatness. Verse 33, in other words, is quite predictable within the story that has developed to this point.

Simeon's second oracle, however, introduces an element of foreboding not previously seen in the birth narrative. The narrator, having described the astonishment of both parents and Simeon's blessing of them, again isolates Mary (as in the responses to the shepherds): "Then [Simeon] said to his mother Mary." Only here does Luke refer to Mary both by name and by reference to her relationship to Jesus. Her name will not appear again until Acts 1:14. This oracle speaks directly to her:

> Behold,
> this one is destined for the fall and the rising of many in Israel
> and as a sign to be spoken against (v. 34b)—
> indeed, your own self a sword will pierce (v. 35a)—
> in order that the inner thoughts of many hearts might be re-
>   vealed. (v. 35b)
>
>   (author's translation)

While Simeon addresses the entire oracle to Mary, the beginning and end focus directly on the significance of Jesus and the role he will play. Jesus is not only to be a "light for revelation to the Gentiles" and "glory to your people Israel," but he also will become a sign of division. His vocation will divide Israel, so that many will fall and rise on his account. He will be the object of resistance and will reveal people's thoughts. The important theme of the rejection of Jesus sounds its first note here, and this ominous note introduces a kind of dissonance against the otherwise joyous and triumphal tone of the birth narrative.

As the Magnificat connects Mary and Israel, so does Simeon's oracle.[22] In the middle of this second oracle, an additional word addresses the future of Mary in particular. Unfortunately, the NRSV reverses the order of the Greek text and obscures this important point. Verses 34b and 35b have to do with the future of the people generally in relationship to Jesus, but v. 35a singles out Mary for comment: "indeed, your own self a sword will pierce." In the long history of reflection on Mary, this saying has understandably aroused a variety of interpretations, some of which are quite fanciful. For example, Origen understood the sword as a reference to Mary's doubt about Jesus' identity during the time of his passion and death.[23] Others have seen in the sword an allusion to Mary's own rejection or her violent death, the harm caused her by allegations of Jesus' illegitimacy, or even the fall of Jerusalem.

Perhaps the interpretation that best accounts for the oracle in its immediate literary context is that of Raymond Brown, who connects the sword with a saying about God's judgment in Ezek 14:17: " 'Let a sword pass through the land'; and I cut off human beings and animals from it." This saying is adapted in the Sibylline Oracles:

> A great affliction will come upon you, Egypt, against your homes,
> a terrible one which you never expected to come upon you,
> for a sword will pass through your midst
> and scattering and death and famine will lay hold of you
> in the seventh generation of kings, and then you will rest.
>   (3:314–18; cf. 3:672–73)[24]

In both texts the saying concerns a sword that selects some for punishment and others for salvation. As such, it could well provide a framework for understanding Luke 2:35a, since in that context also a separation is being made between those who either fall or rise because of Jesus. In Luke 12:51–53 Jesus insists that such a discrimination occurs even within families. By directing this saying to Mary, the oracle hints that even being a member of Jesus' own family does not shield Mary from the discrimination that lies ahead.[25]

This interpretation of the sword that pierces Mary as the sword of discrimination fits well within the immediate context, but it does not exhaust the possible meanings of the saying, and a saying may well bear more than a single point within the overall story. For example, in Acts 2:39 Peter announces that the promise of the gospel is "for you, for your children, and for all who are far away." The immediate context suggests that even "those who are far away" are Jews who are presently removed from Jerusalem, but within the larger Lukan story, the promise extends to include Gentiles as well. In this same way, this particular oracle, with its vivid image of the sword piercing Mary, also at least hints at the pain the death of Jesus will cause her.

Greco-Roman letters of consolation often employ the imagery of a sword in discussion of the grief of mothers upon the loss of a child. Seneca, for example, writes to his mother about her loss as a result of his own exile:

> Of all the wounds that have ever gone deep into your body, this latest one, I admit, is the most serious; it has not merely torn the outer skin, but pierced your very breast and vitals. But just as raw recruits cry out even when they are slightly wounded, and shudder more at the hands of the surgeons than they do at the sword, while veterans, though deeply wounded, submit patiently and without a groan to the cleansing of their festered bodies just as if these were not their own, so now you ought to offer yourself bravely to be healed. (*To Helvia on Consolation* 3.1)[26]

In another letter of consolation, Seneca uses the same imagery:

> that you may know that even this deep-cut wound will surely heal, I have shown you the scar of an old wound that was not less severe. (*To Marcia on Consolation* 1.5; cf. 1.8)[27]

In a discussion of Arria, who kept knowledge of their son's death from her husband because he himself was gravely ill, Pliny describes what he regards as her exemplary behavior:

> When she found she could no longer restrain her grief, but her tears were gushing out, she would leave the room, and having given vent to her passion, return again with dry eyes and a serene countenance, as if she had dismissed every pang of bereavement at her entrance. The action was, no doubt, truly noble, when drawing the dagger she plunged it into her breast, and then presented it to her husband with that ever-memorable, I had almost said that divine expression, "It does not hurt, my Paetus." It must however be considered, when she spoke and acted thus, that she had the prospect of immortal glory before her eyes to encourage and support her. But was it not something much greater, without the view of such powerful motives, to

> hide her tears, to conceal her grief, and cheerfully play the
> mother when she was so no more? (*Letters* 3.16)[28]

While these and other instances in which grief, particularly a mother's grief, is compared with a wound, do not constitute a stock literary feature, they do suggest that the piercing of Mary at least *includes* the pain involved in the death of Jesus.[29] Objections to this interpretation arise from the fact that Luke does not place Mary at the crucifixion; thus there is no direct evidence for Mary as *mater dolorosa* in the Third Gospel.[30] But Mary's absence at the crucifixion does not mean that it does not concern her or that Luke is unaware of its implications for her. The piercing by the sword does not have to be fulfilled in a direct fashion within the narrative, so that the reader "sees" the pain of Mary in a specific event. (For that matter, the reader also does not "see" the division of Mary's family regarding Jesus.) That Mary is not present at the cross is not itself particularly significant.

The foreboding element that enters the birth narrative in Simeon's oracle concerns both the resistance to Jesus that will eventually lead to his death and the implications of that death for "Mary, his mother." In this scene Mary acquires a third role. In addition to her earlier roles as disciple and prophet, here she takes on the role of mother. Of course, the birth of Jesus itself literally makes her a mother and the aftermath of the shepherds' visit finds her "pondering" the meaning of what has occurred, but this scene confirms her role as mother even as it foreshadows Jesus' death and hints at her grief.

Following the appearance of Simeon is the much briefer prophecy of Anna. Her thanksgiving for the birth of Jesus complements that of Simeon and brings the entire scene to a close on a more positive note than that provided by Simeon's second oracle. In addition, the age of Anna, like that of Elizabeth, contrasts with the youth of Mary, as does the narrator's note about her long years as a widow. The identification of Anna's father and tribe again recalls the many things left unsaid about the mother of Jesus. While Elizabeth and Anna together recall numerous women in Israel's history, they serve also as foils for Mary, indicating not only her youth but also the inexplicable nature of her selection by God.

Jesus in the Temple

Forming the conclusion to the infancy narrative, this episode serves in part to show, rather than merely to tell, what the narrator has asserted in 2:40 and will again assert in 2:52, namely, that Jesus grows and matures in the eyes of God as well as of human beings (compare the notice about John the Baptist in 1:80). This final episode in the Lukan birth narrative also employs Mary to continue and even enhance the narrative tension introduced with Mary's "pondering" in 2:19 and with the oracle about a sword piercing Mary in 2:35.

The episode opens with an explanation that "his parents" customarily went to Jerusalem each year for the feast of Passover. In addition to setting the stage for the events that follow, this notice again focuses attention on Jerusalem, attention that Luke will continue throughout both the Gospel and Acts, and reinforces the impression of the faithfulness of the parents of Jesus. The verses that follow describe how the parents start out for home, only to realize that Jesus is not among the people who are traveling together and, therefore, they return to Jerusalem. The actions of Mary and Joseph, referred to here by the collective "his parents," dominate the early part of this story. Thirteen verbs have them as their subject, for it is Mary and Joseph whose actions constitute the movement in this episode: "they started to return . . . [they] did not know. . . . they went. . . . they started to look. . . . they did not find . . . they returned to Jerusalem to search. . . . they found. . . . his parents saw him . . . they were astonished. . . ." Apart from the reference to Jesus' staying behind in Jerusalem in verse 43, every action in the story prior to their discovery of Jesus is an action of the parents.

The discovery of Jesus in the temple prompts two responses. First, those who are gathered there ("all who heard him") are amazed by him (*existēmi*, v. 47). Second, "his parents" echo this amazement with their own; they are overwhelmed (*ekplēssein*, v. 48; cf. 4:32, 9:43).[31] But it is Mary who speaks, her response being distinguished once again from that of others (2:18–19, 34–35), even from that of "the parents": "Child, why did you act this way to us? Behold, your father and I have been looking for you in anguish" (author's translation).

Often interpreters move quickly past this saying, and the reasons for that are understandable. For many Christians, the notion that Mary chastises Jesus causes serious theological problems, since Gabriel's annunciation about Jesus' birth might be thought to inform her of his unique status. Critical biblical scholarship, with its customary preoccupation with the history behind the text, has moved past this saying for a different set of reasons. There is some agreement that this entire episode was written independently of the bulk of the Lukan birth narrative and only later attached to it. As an episode that might have circulated separately, it reflects an interest in the boyhood of Jesus such as develops more extensively in the apocryphal gospels. As long as questions about the history behind narratives and the history of the narrative stood in the foreground of discussion, scholars seldom puzzled over Mary's revealing question, but that question plays an interesting role in the birth narrative as a whole.

In the first place, the question, or question and assertion, singles out
Mary. As one of "the parents," she has been actively seeking her son and now
has found him. Commentators often point to the cultural inappropriateness of
Mary's question, since it would be the father's duty to chastise his son. Often
Mary's question is attributed solely to the fact that Jesus is about to refer to
God as his father, but that interpretation overlooks the Lukan pattern of identi-
fying Mary's responses throughout the infancy narrative.[32]

The statement "Behold, your father and I have been looking for you in
anguish" not only identifies their actions, as has already been done by the
narrator, but it also identifies their emotions. Although the birth narrative
abounds in what might be called emotional responses to various angelic
announcements (1:29, 65; 2:9), and although it hints at the pain Mary will
feel at Jesus' death, the emotional claim Mary makes here is of a different
sort. This is not the stereotypical response of amazement in the presence of
divine activity, nor is it a foreboding about the future. It is the real and
present terror of parents who do not know where their child is.

The NRSV's bland translation ("your father and I have been searching
for you in great anxiety") fails to capture the poignancy of the word Luke
selects *(odynoun)*, but some prominent instances of its usage in the Septuagint (the Greek translation of the Old Testament) will illustrate its force. In
the book of Tobit, Tobias insists to his new father-in-law, who delays Tobias's return to his family, that he must return home: "For you know that my
father must be counting the days, and if I delay even one day I will upset
him very much" *(odynoun, 9:4)*. There follows the story of Tobit's anguish
over his son's delay and his mother's conviction that she would never see
Tobit again. 4 Maccabees 8–18 details the story of a widow who is killed
by Antiochus for her faithfulness to the traditions of Israel, but only after
she has witnessed the martyrdoms of all of her seven sons. She rejoices that
her husband did not experience her own anguish *(odynoun)* over the death
of her sons (4 Macc 18:9; cf. the version in 2 Maccabees 7). Mary's comment to Jesus once again portrays her in the role of mother, a mother whose
search is accompanied by nothing less than anguish.

Mary's question and rebuke of Jesus also introduce conflict into the
story, as is evident from the fact that Jesus responds with a question, just as
he will later respond to undeniably hostile interrogators (e.g., 6:1–5, 6–11;
14:1–6).[33] While the Greek leaves it unclear whether Jesus refers to his
father's "business" or "things" or "house," he does distinguish himself from
his "parents" by invoking his obligation to his "father." And the question
that he asks in no way responds to Mary's concern. Indeed, it may be understood as a *rejection* of her question, perhaps even of her prerogative to ask
a question.[34] The narrator's comment that "they did not understand what he
said to them" only reinforces the wedge this episode drives between Jesus

and Mary (and Joseph). Like other episodes in the birth narrative, this one concludes with a notice about going away (cf. 1:23, 38, 56; 2:20, 39). Jesus leaves Jerusalem and returns to Nazareth with his parents. The additional note that Jesus was obedient or submissive to them serves to alleviate, for the time being, the tension introduced by Mary's rebuke.

At the conclusion of both the episode and the entire birth narrative stand two brief comments by the narrator. The second, concerning the growth and evaluation of Jesus, parallels the statement about John the Baptist in 1:80 (cf. 2:40). Taken together, the two round off the story that begins in 1:5 and prepare the reader for further evidence of the "wisdom" and the "years" of these two figures.

By contrast, the narrator's first concluding comment concerns Mary and provides not a "conclusion" at all but instead an element of *in*conclusion: "His mother kept all these things in her heart" (author's translation). Since the return home brings an end to the temple scene, "all these things" refers not only to what happened there but may include everything that has occurred since the annunciation of Gabriel. And, unless we take this to be a very pedestrian comment about the way in which tradition concerning Jesus' birth arose (i.e., Mary remembered things and passed them on to the archivist), then the comment reflects the unfinished nature of what Mary has witnessed. Just as Joseph's story is only beginning when Jacob is said to keep things in his heart (Gen 37:11), Mary's act is not one of mere memory but of reflection and anticipation.

The narrator leaves quite unclear what exactly Mary may be anticipating, and only by neglecting important threads in the story may we assume that she anticipates Jesus' role with complete understanding and acceptance. Having read her word of submission to the angelic announcement, her prophetic praise of God, Simeon's oracle concerning the sword that threatens her, her rebuke of Jesus and inability to understand him, the reader puzzles not only over Jesus and his future but over Mary herself. Where will she stand in relationship to the child whose birth she accepted?

MARY IN THE MINISTRY OF JESUS
(LUKE 8:19–21, 11:27–28)

Zechariah, Elizabeth, and Joseph stay behind in the nativity scene, leaving Mary as the only adult who appears in both the Lukan birth narrative and elsewhere in the Lukan Gospel.[35] "Appears" is the correct verb in this instance, since Luke refers to her directly in a single brief episode (8:19–21), though without using her name even there, and indirectly in one other episode (11:27–28).

Luke 8:19–21

The first episode describes "his mother and his brothers" coming to see Jesus and being unable to reach him because of the crowd. When Jesus is told that they are standing outside, he replies: "My mother and my brothers—these are the ones who hear the word of God and do it" (8:21, author's translation). Because this episode appears also in Mark (3:31–35), most discussion of it has focused on the changes Luke introduces in the earlier Markan form of the story. In response to the same report that his mother and brothers wish to see him, the Markan Jesus replies: "Who are my mother and my brothers?" Looking at those about him, he adds: "Behold, my mother and my brothers! Whoever does the will of God—this one is my brother, and sister, and mother" (Mark 3:33–35, author's translation). The Markan saying leaves Jesus' family on the outside as he looks about on those whom he calls his family. By omitting the question of Jesus ("Who are my mother and my brothers?") and by omitting the explicit identification of those around him as his family, Luke at least "softens" this implied rejection of the biological family of Jesus (cf. Matt 12:46–50). These changes lead some interpreters to conclude that Luke not only "softens" the Markan portrait of Jesus' family, but he elevates them to the position of "models for those who hear the word of God and keep it." [36]

As it appears in Luke, Jesus' saying is quite ambiguous. "My mother and my brothers—these are the ones who hear the word of God and do it." This saying *could* mean that Jesus' mother and brothers are among those who respond to God's words in faith, but it *can also* mean that Jesus' true family, *as distinct from* his physical family, consists of those who respond to God's words. Translation alone will not resolve this ambiguity.

Attention to the narrative context of the saying will help to underscore its ambiguity. The visit of Mary and Jesus' brothers occurs just after Jesus tells the parable of the sower, the interpretation of which emphasizes varying responses to God's word (8:11–15). Jesus tells the parable to "a great crowd," but to his disciples he explains that they alone are to know the "secrets of the kingdom of God." In other words, the parable and its interpretation highlight the distinction between those who are "insiders" and those who are "outsiders."

Since Jesus' mother and brothers come to him just *after* the telling of the parable, they apparently do not belong with those who "know the secrets." They are not disciples. But Luke comments that "they could not reach him because of the crowd," which also distinguishes Jesus' family from the crowd, suggesting that they also are not to be regarded as outsiders. They stand at the boundary between the two groups, neither in nor out. Jesus' ambiguous comment about his (true) mother and brothers, then, leaves their position entirely unclear. Following the parable, in fact, this episode would seem to raise the question: among which "seed" are the mother and brothers?

Luke does not present this incident as a rejection of Mary, but he also does not here portray her as the ideal disciple. What this incident does do is raise a question about Mary's position vis-à-vis Jesus. Is she an insider or an outsider? The narrative tension that Luke introduces in the birth narrative re-emerges, not yet to be resolved.

Before leaving this text, it is appropriate to comment on the presence here of "brothers" of Jesus. For our purposes, this reference is important primarily because it connects Mary with other family members and introduces figures who will take on a significant role in Acts. The question whether these are brothers of Jesus or half-brothers or other male relatives arises not only because of the Greek word itself *(adelphoi)* but also because of traditional views of the perpetual virginity of Mary *(aeiparthenos)*.[37]

Luke 11:27–28

The brief exchange between Jesus and an unnamed woman in 11:27–28 scarcely resolves the ambiguity of 8:19–21. When the woman cries out to Jesus, "Blessed is the womb that bore you and the breasts that nursed you," Jesus responds, "Blessed rather are those who hear the word of God and obey it!" The woman's blessing recalls and begins to fulfill Mary's words in the Magnificat: "from now on all generations will call me blessed." This recollection, however, reveals nothing of Luke's assessment of Mary, since both in the Magnificat and in the woman's cry the blessing focuses attention on Jesus and his greatness. Mary herself comes into view only as the recipient of God's gracious blessing.

Interpreters have argued diametrically opposing readings of Jesus' response. Some have taken the saying to mean that Mary is among those who "hear and keep the word of God," but others see in the saying another rejection of the biological mother. Such conflict in interpretation arises again from the *ambiguity* of the saying and its context. As in 8:19–21, it is simply unclear whether Mary belongs among those Jesus blesses.

MARY IN THE CHURCH (ACTS 1:14)

In Acts Luke refers to Mary a single time. Following the ascension, Luke describes how the apostles return to Jerusalem and gather in the upper room. He then lists the names of the eleven and follows the list with a comment: "All these were constantly devoting themselves to prayer, together with certain women, including Mary the mother of Jesus, as well as his brothers" (1:14).

With this brief reference to Mary, Luke resolves the tension regarding Mary that he introduced in the birth narrative. Neither the "sword" that threatened her nor her own inability to understand Jesus prevented her from becoming one of those gathered in the upper room. That these are the ones who are faithful to the "word of God" there can be scarcely a doubt. Mary, who begins in Luke's story as a disciple (Luke 1:38), appears here also as a disciple. The later appearances of Jesus' brothers may serve to remind the reader of her position.

The resolution of the tension regarding Mary appropriately occurs at this spot in Luke's overall narrative. Mary's unique place in the birth narrative carries over into Jesus' ministry and into this time of transition into the early church, but she does not figure in the emerging church of Jerusalem and beyond. Nevertheless, as Luke portrays here the gathering and strengthening of the central members of the community, it is essential that he include Mary among that number, for she is the only figure who is present both in the prologue to the gospel and in the prologue to the church. Especially in view of Jesus' ascension in Acts 1:9–11, and therefore his absence from the community, Mary's presence connects this story with all that has preceded.

CONCLUSION

What has this reading of the relevant passages revealed about Mary as a character in Luke-Acts? That question may still seem an odd one, particularly if we think of characterization along the lines of Trollope introducing each new figure within his narrative or the profound psychological portraits employed in contemporary novels. Characterization, however, need not involve explicit and extensive discussion of the traits of an individual. It may be, and indeed often is, accomplished by means of a character's actions, juxtaposition with other characters, and place within the larger development of the narrative.

The Roles of Mary

Even in these short episodes, Luke presents Mary in three distinct but interrelated roles. In response to Gabriel's annunciation of Jesus' birth, Mary appears as a disciple, perhaps even as the first disciple. Her affirmation, "Behold, the slave of the Lord. Let it be to me according to your word," provides her assent to the gospel. Elizabeth's praise of her confidence in God's word reinforces this role of Mary as a true disciple. While Luke later on introduces tension about Mary and her status as a disciple, that tension is finally resolved in her unambiguous presence in the upper room.

If Mary is first and foremost a disciple of Jesus, that is not her only role in Luke-Acts. In the powerful words of the Magnificat, she becomes not only a disciple but also a prophet. With imagery of God exalting the lowly and humbling the mighty, Mary's words recall prominent prophetic themes and anticipate the presence of those same themes in Jesus' sermon at Nazareth. By identifying God's action in her own case with the promises to the fathers, Mary locates the Christ event firmly within the history of Israel.

Mary's third role in Luke-Acts, that of mother, appears to be her most direct and obvious, but in fact it emerges as the most complex. Luke provides only a lean description of the actual birth of Jesus, the point at which Mary becomes a mother. The story provides scant glorification of Mary, since its focus everywhere is the baby rather than the mother. And yet at several points Luke distinguishes Mary and her response to events from others who are also present. Mary is the one who ponders the things that have happened (2:19, 2:51). It is Mary's soul that will be pierced (2:35). It is Mary who announces her anguish over the disappearance of Jesus following the Passover trip to Jerusalem (2:48). These brief notices serve several functions in the narrative, one of which is to capture the very normal attachment of mother to child.

While I have distinguished these three roles from one another in order to clarify each of them, they are in fact significantly connected with one another. Unless we see all of these, we will once again flatten Mary's character and reduce her to a single feature or one function.

This discussion has intentionally used the term "role" in order to describe Mary's place (or places) in the narrative and has deliberately avoided referring to Mary as a "type" or a "symbol." My reasons for that choice of terminology are largely pragmatic. Too often, when Mary becomes a "symbol" or a "type" she is understood to be a "symbol" of all women or a "type" of true motherhood. I shall leave the task of explaining that tendency to students of the history of religions and the psychology of religion, but it does seem significant that men who appear in biblical stories are seldom, if ever, taken to be the type of all males or symbolic of all males. Certainly Luke gives no indication that he regards Mary as a type or symbol confined to women. Indeed, if Mary is a symbol at all, she symbolizes God's gift of grace to all humankind.

One additional issue regarding Mary's roles in Luke-Acts deserves a brief comment at this point, and that is the complaint sometimes made that Mary is a passive figure. While Luke says more about Mary than does any other New

Testament writer, she nevertheless remains passive and, hence, has been seen as reinforcing the supposed passivity of women. In a sense, Mary does here remain a passive figure. God's messenger appears to her, God chooses to use her body, she remains a witness to events rather than an actor in them. However, to emphasize this passivity in and of itself is to distort Luke's theology. Part of his perspective, indeed a large part, is that God is in control of events and God has shaped what has happened among us (Luke 1:1). While Mary appears to be passive, the same could be said of most characters in Luke-Acts. And in some important ways Mary is not a passive character. Our reading of the story has demonstrated the way in which her action ties together significant pieces of the narrative (2:6–7, 41–51). In fact, we have seen that the responses of Mary and to Mary run through this story and give shape to what is otherwise simply a list of events.

Mary and Narrative Development

The discussion of Mary's roles within Luke-Acts may leave the impression that these are static parts that Mary plays, one at one point and another at a different point in the story. In the discussion of literary characterization in chapter 1 above, however, I argued for a more fluid understanding of characterization, one that would ask how a given character intersects with the development of the narrative.

We have seen that, in the birth narrative, Mary becomes the major bearer for the elements of foreboding that are introduced. In the midst of a story that proclaims the arrival of Jesus as "son of the Most High" and heir of David's throne, Luke sounds a note of the forthcoming rejection of Jesus and the division he will bring. Simeon makes that announcement, but he makes it to Mary, and part of it addresses her alone (2:34–35). Similarly, the anguished rebuke of the youthful Jesus who stays behind in the temple hints at other rebukes that will also follow (2:48). Mary becomes the bearer for these forebodings of the rejection that lies ahead.

This sense of foreboding participates in a larger set of narrative tensions. What makes any story worth telling or reading is the unresolved tension (or tensions) along the way: Will the boy finally get the girl (or vice versa)? Will the murderer be caught? Will Paul make it to Rome in order to preach the gospel there? In addition to this type of narrative tension, which becomes the focal point for a story, there are smaller tensions that move the story along. In Acts, one of these tensions arises when Paul is converted and has to do with whether the disciples in Jerusalem will accept him. Another of the minor tensions in Luke-Acts, as we have seen, involves Mary. Is she to remain a disciple of the Lord, as in Luke 1:38, or will her inability to understand Jesus and even her concern for him prevent her from remaining within the circle? That question, first sounded at the end of the birth narrative, remains unanswered throughout the gospel. Her appearance in Luke 8:19–21 continues the ambiguity. Only when she joins those in the upper room in Acts 1:14 does the tension find resolution: Mary is a disciple.

Mary and the Order of Luke-Acts

One of the tasks of a narrative, whether understood to be history or fiction, is to give or create order. In the introductory discussion of characterization, I drew upon Springer's discussion of the "governing principle" of a work of fiction, but works of history also have such principles. Without them, there would be only a string of scenes, and even a text so organized may be shown to rely on an underlying principle.[38] In studying characterization in a work, this point leads to the question of how a given character is connected with the underlying principle or order of the whole.

The order of Luke-Acts is the subject of ongoing critical discussion that need not be rehearsed here. Within that order, at least one of the major components is Luke's understanding that the "events that have been fulfilled among us" have to do with nothing less than God's salvation of all people, both the Gentiles and the people of Israel. This understanding of salvation, so prominent in the birth narrative, recurs again and again, even in the closing lines of Acts (28:28). Luke's story is a story of God's salvation of all people. In one sense, Mary's role in Luke's ordering of events simply derives from the fact that she is Jesus' mother. In another sense, however, Mary is among the first to receive God's salvation, for Gabriel's proclamation, "you have found favor with God," accompanied by no description of Mary's virtues and antedating her obedience to God, comes as pure grace. Mary knows of God's salvation not only through herself but also for herself.

NOTES

1. I follow the convention of referring to the author of the Gospel of Luke and the Acts of the Apostles as Luke, without suggesting thereby any particular identification of that author.

2. Technically, of course, what we are after is the understanding of the implied author, since we have no access to the actual historical author; and there may be differences between the actual author's view of a character and the view assumed by the implied author. In the case of Luke, however, there is no reason to suspect a conflict between the two. On the term *implied author* see Wayne Booth, *The Rhetoric of Fiction* (2nd ed.; Chicago: University of Chicago Press, 1983) esp. 71–76.

3. *The Theology of St. Luke,* trans. Geoffrey Buswell (New York: Harper and Row, 1961) esp. 18 n.1, 22 n.2, 118, 172.

4. Brown, *The Birth of the Messiah* (updated edition; New York: Doubleday, 1993) 479.

5. Brown, *Birth,* 250–53; see also R. Laurentin, *Structure et Théologie de Luc I– II* (Paris: Gabalda, 1957) 23–33; H. Wayne Merritt applies a structualist analysis to the same parallels in "The Angel's Announcement: A Structuralist Study," in *Text and Logos: The Humanistic Interpretation of the New Testament,* ed. Theodore W. Jennings, Jr. (Homage Series; Atlanta: Scholars, 1990) 97–108.

6. In Matt 25:1, 7, 11 and Acts 21:9, *parthenos* refers to a young unmarried woman, without attention to the question of biological virginity. See also the usage in Pausanias 8.20.4 (*Description of Greece,* trans. W. H. S. Jones [LCL; 6 vols.; London: Heinemann, 1933] 3:438–39); Diodorus Siculus 20.84.3 (*Diodorus of Sicily,* trans. R. Geer [LCL; 12 vols.; Cambridge: Harvard University Press, 1954] 10:362–63); Lycophron 1141, 1175 (*Callimachus and Lycophron,* trans. A. W. Mair [LCL; London: Heinemann, 1955] pp. 414–15, 416–17); Sophocles, *Oedipus Rex,* 1462. In Sophocles' *Women of Trachis,* the dying Heracles urges his son to marry the *parthenos* of King Eurytus, who has already been Heracles' mistress (1216–29), a clear instance in which *parthenos* cannot refer to someone who is without sexual experience (*Sophocles,* trans. F. Storr [LCL; 2 vols.; Cambridge: Harvard University Press, 1912–13] 1:132–33, 2:354–55).

7. There is some ambiguity in the Greek at this point; the phrase "from the house of David" could refer either to Mary or to Joseph. Word order, as well as the notice in 2:4, argues for understanding the phrase to describe Joseph.

8. On this phrase see the article by W. C. van Unnik, "*Dominus vobiscum:* The Background of a Liturgical Formula," in *New Testament Essays: Studies in Memory of Thomas Walter Manson,* ed. A. J. B. Higgins (Manchester: Manchester University Press, 1959) 270–305.

9. See the summary of the debate by Brown (*Birth,* 298–309), whose conclusion is similar to my own.

10. Brown, *Birth,* 315.

11. BAGD, 205–6. A number of other modern translations also read "servant" (for example, NJB, NEB, TEV, NIV, and REB). Other translations include "handmaid" (RSV, JB, and NAB) and "maidservant" (NKJV).

12. Brown, *Birth,* 319.

13. As the footnote in the NRSV indicates, a few early manuscripts of Luke attribute the Magnificat to Elizabeth rather than to Mary. This attribution gave rise to great controversy roughly a century ago. However, both internal and external factors incline me to regard Mary as the speaker.

14. See the chart in Brown, *Birth,* 357–59.

15. Brown, *Birth,* 365.

16. See, for example, Luke Timothy Johnson, *The Gospel of Luke* (Sacra Pagina 3; Collegeville, Minn.: Liturgical, 1991) 43.

17. See the good brief introduction to Luke's use of prophecy in Johnson, *Gospel of Luke,* 15–21.

18. I am grateful to Frank Matera for this suggestion regarding Mary's presence at Pentecost and its relationship to the Magnificat.

19. In this paragraph I expand on an insight of Ben F. Meyer, " 'But Mary Kept All These Things . . .' (Lk 2, 19.51)," *CBQ* 26 (1964) 46.

20. The verb translated "kept" in the NRSV is *diatēroun* in the LXX; compare the closely related word *syntēroun* in Luke 2:19.

21. Brown, *Birth*, 447–51.

22. Johnson, *The Gospel of Luke*, 56–57.

23. *In Lucan Homilia* XVII (*PG* 13:1845–46).

24. "The Sibylline Oracles," trans. J. J. Collins, in J. H. Charlesworth, ed. *The Old Testament Pseudepigrapha* (2 vols.; Garden City, N.Y.: Doubleday, 1983, 1985) 1:369.

25. Brown, *Birth*, 462–66; so also Joseph A. Fitzmyer, *The Gospel According to Luke* (AB 28; 2 vols.; Garden City, N.Y.: Doubleday, 1981, 1985) 1:429–30.

26. *Seneca: Moral Essays*, trans. John W. Basore (LCL; 3 vols.; Cambridge: Harvard University Press, 1928–35) 2:423.

27. Ibid., 2:7.

28. Pliny, *Letters*, trans. William Melmoth (LCL; 2 vols.; London: Heinemann, 1915) 1:246–49. The incident referred to is Arria's decision to die with her husband when he is forced to commit suicide (see Martial 1.13 [*Epigrams*, trans. W. C. A. Ker (2 vols.; LCL; London: Heinemann, 1919) 1:39]).

29. Note also Plutarch, *Moralia* 610B (*Plutarch's Moralia*, vol. 7: trans. Phillip H. DeLacy and Benedict Einarson [LCL; Cambridge: Harvard University Press, 1959] 592–93) and Artemidorus, 1.14–15 (*Artemidori Daldiana Onirocriticon Liber v*, ed. Roger A. Pack [Bibliotheca scriptorum graecorum et romanorum teubneriana; Leipzig: Teubner, 1963] 39, 19).

30. Brown, *Birth*, 462; Fitzmyer, *Luke*, 1:429.

31. Technically, verse 48 says only that "they" were overwhelmed. The context, however, makes it clear that "they" refers to Jesus' parents, since those who are present in the temple with Jesus have already registered their amazement.

32. François Bovon, for example, sees Mary's question simply as a way of drawing attention to the opposition between Jesus' two fathers (*Das Evangelium nach Lukas: Lk 1,1–9,50* [EKKNT; Zurich: Benziger, 1989] 158–59). By contrast, Heikki Räisänen argues that both Luke 2:41–52 and John 2:1–12 are early commentaries on the distance between Jesus and his mother posited in Mark 3:31–35 (*Die Mutter Jesu im Neuen Testament* [Helsinki: Suomalainen Tiedeakatemia, 1969] 134–35).

33. Indeed, form critically, this would appear to be a controversy apophthegm, a dialogue in which some act of Jesus prompts a critical question to him and then a saying in reply.

34. See the same pattern in Acts 1:6–11, where the disciples' questions are answered in ways that essentially reject the questions.

35. Brown, *Birth*, 429.

36. Fitzmyer, *Luke*, 1:725.

37. See the discussion of perpetual virginity above, pp. 12 and 15; on the brothers of Jesus, see John P. Meier, *A Marginal Jew: Rethinking the Historical Jesus,*

vol. 1: *The Roots of the Problem and the Person* (New York: Doubleday, 1991) 318–32, and Fitzmyer, *Luke,* 1:723–25.

38. On this point see the important essay of Hayden White "The Value of Narrativity in the Representation of Reality," in *The Content of the Form: Narrative Discourse and Historical Representation* (Baltimore: Johns Hopkins University Press, 1987) 1–25.

CHAPTER 4

Cana and the Cross
The Mother of Jesus in the Gospel of John

Jesus
the man alone
seeing his mother
in the midst of the mocking and jeering
cries
Woman, this is your son

What a wedding feast this is—
that he calls her 'Woman' once more
What a wedding this is—
her Son hanging on a gibbet between two criminals—yet alone
Alan Falconer, A Man Alone

In the Gospel of John, the treatment of Jesus' mother departs significantly from what we have found in Luke and Matthew, where Mary figures primarily in stories of the birth and infancy of Jesus. John never even uses the name Mary, calling her instead "the mother of Jesus" and "his mother." When Jesus himself speaks to her, it is with the enigmatic address "Woman." She appears twice, near the beginning of the Gospel and again near its end (although the fact that people know both Jesus' father and mother is referred to in 6:42; cf. 8:41, which may refer to rumors about Jesus' birth). In the first scene involving Jesus' mother, a wedding feast at Cana, the mother's words provide the occasion for Jesus' first miracle. In the second, she stands near the cross. Neither scene has a counterpart in the synoptic Gospels.

The distinctiveness of John's treatment of Jesus' mother ought not be surprising, since John's Gospel stands apart from the synoptics in many aspects of its style and content.[1] Because most contemporary readers come to John aware of the infancy narratives of Luke and Matthew, however, the absence of such a narrative here raises a number of questions. Are we to infer that the evangelist is unaware of the stories about Jesus' miraculous conception? Or, perhaps more troublesome, does John find those stories somehow problematic or offensive? These questions are part of a larger complex of questions concerning the literary and historical relationships between John and the synoptic Gospels, questions concerning which scholarly agreement is notably lacking.[2] Because this study of the characterization of Mary concerns the narratives as we have them, that is, the final stage of gospel composition, such questions lie beyond our scope. As with our exploration of Mary's role or roles in Matthew and in Luke, our concern here is how Mary (in this case referred to as "the mother of Jesus") emerges as a literary character.

It could be supposed that John's virtual silence regarding Mary might yield a comparable silence on the part of exegetes, but the importance as well as the difficulties of the two scenes in which she does appear have led to numerous attempts at explaining the significance of Jesus' mother in this Gospel. Indeed, interpretations of Mary in John's Gospel range widely— even wildly. For some, the mother of Jesus in John's Gospel symbolizes the church, for others the new Eve, Jewish Christianity, or the Lady Zion. Others regard all such symbolic interpretation as capricious and insist that Mary's role is restricted to that of mere functionary in service of the plot. In the Cana scene, she prompts the miracle, and at the cross she appears only because John wishes to demonstrate the filial affection of Jesus himself. There is no symbolic importance to be attached to her in either case.

Given such diversity of interpretation, a fresh approach to the question of Mary's role may be needed. One such approach emerges if we ask how these scenes would strike us if some other person appeared in them, instead of "the mother of Jesus." If some otherwise unknown Salome approached Jesus with the news that there was no more wine for the wedding celebration, and if that same Salome stood at the cross with the Beloved Disciple, what significance would we attach to her? I suspect that we would understand Salome primarily as a literary and theological connection between these two scenes, for a number of features connect the two, as we shall see. Beyond that, we would probably not search for profound theological symbolism in the person of Salome.

Such a conclusion does not mean, however, that "the mother of Jesus" in John's Gospel is but a literary-theological device without any significance of her own: John does not refer to our character as "Salome" or even as "Mary," but as "the mother of Jesus," thus raising the question of what special meaning John attaches to that phrase. The context suggests, as we shall see, that "the mother of Jesus" is among John's ways of recalling that Jesus was a human being. That is, "the mother of Jesus" underscores the fact—the paradox—that the Johannine Jesus, who comes "from above," is at the same time a human being whose earthly father and mother and brothers and geographical origin are known.

"THE MOTHER OF JESUS WAS THERE" (JOHN 2:1–12)

The story of Jesus transforming water into wine contains so many incongruities and raises so many questions that we need to acknowledge from the beginning what a challenge it has posed to interpreters. The great majority of Jesus' miracles involve Jesus in fulfilling some basic human need, whether for healing or for food or for safety (in a storm, for example). By astonishing contrast, in this miracle Jesus supplies a vast quantity of wine for a wedding feast. That Jesus should be the purveyor of wine led some earlier interpreters to regard this event as "inappropriate" and to question its historicity on the grounds that Jesus would surely not be indulging in mere pleasure or, worse yet, keeping company with drunkards.[3] It is not only on moralistic grounds that interpreters have found this story difficult, however. The stage for the miracle is set by what is, on any reading, an awkward exchange between Jesus and his mother. The narrator does not directly describe the miracle itself but forces us to infer it from the action that takes place. And, unlike most of Jesus' miracles, the bystanders do not respond with awe or amazement to an action of Jesus; instead, the steward greets with some astonishment what he takes to be the action of the bridegroom. Only in light of the whole of John's Gospel can some features of this story be understood—and some will remain unexplained—for the story hints at events that lie ahead rather than prosaically announcing a program that will mechanically unfold.

In order to see how this story works, it is important to attend to its connections with the earlier parts of the narrative. The Cana story is often treated in isolation from the narrative that precedes, largely because the narrator identifies the miracle as the first of Jesus' signs (v. 11) and therefore connects it with the miracles that follow, but the connections backward are also significant. References to Jesus' mother and brothers in 2:1–12 connect this event back to earlier references to his home in Nazareth (1:45–46) and to his father, Joseph (1:45). This web of references to Jesus' physical family and geographical place seems to conflict with the prologue to John's Gospel (1:1–18), which identifies the subject of the Gospel that follows as the Logos, the Word of God. The prologue speaks of this Logos as life and light, as the glory of God, and as the conveyer of grace to human beings. With the possible exception of 1:14, however, little in the prologue causes us to anticipate that the Logos will enter the narrative as a real, flesh-and-blood human being.[4] Only in 1:30, when John the Baptist identifies Jesus as a "man" (Greek, *anēr*), does the reader have a clear indication that the Logos is human. Within that scene and the following one, in which two of John's disciples follow Jesus, Jesus is identified as "Lamb of God," "man," "Son of God," "rabbi," and "Messiah." Several of these terms connect Jesus with the Logos figure of the prologue, but they convey to the reader little of his human connections. Nothing has been said about Jesus' birth, family, or place of origin.

The scene in which Jesus meets Philip and Nathanael (1:43–51) begins to fill in vital information about Jesus. In Philip's announcement to Nathanael about "Jesus son of Joseph from Nazareth," we learn the name of Jesus' father. In the same statement and in Nathanael's skeptical question, "Can anything good come out of Nazareth?" we learn the place of Jesus' origins (at least Jesus' earthly origins). Moreover, this scene is the first to occur in Galilee (1:43), linking its location with the wedding at Cana that follows (see 2:1, 11).

Given the reference to Jesus' father and hometown, and the reference to Jesus' brothers in 2:12, the appearance of Jesus' mother in 2:1 is not as abrupt as it might at first glance appear. It occurs, in fact, within a small network of references to Jesus' relatives and his home. The Logos is not a disembodied spirit, after all, but has family and location just as does any other flesh-and-blood human being. Jesus is simultaneously God's only son and the son of Mary and Joseph.[5]

The scene opens by first placing the mother of Jesus at the wedding (2:1) and only then Jesus and his disciples (2:2). Since she is referred to again in 2:3 and speaks before Jesus does, we might suppose that the narrator is drawing our attention to the mother of Jesus as an important figure, but this introduction is in fact similar to those of other Johannine stories. The story of Jesus' nocturnal conversation with Nicodemus begins by identifying Nicodemus and relaying his initial words to Jesus (3:1–2). The healing of the royal official's son begins similarly, with an identification of the man and then a description of his begging Jesus for help (4:46–47; cf. 5:5, 11:1). The initial reference to Jesus' mother, then, conforms to a normal Johannine pattern, except that the narrator *tells the reader less about Jesus' mother than about anyone else*. Other characters are at least described—"a leader of the Jews" or "a man . . . who had been ill for thirty-eight years." Of this woman we know only that she is Jesus' mother.

That knowledge receives little or no amplification in the story that follows. In verse 3 the narrator explains that the wine has run out, and the mother of Jesus then speaks to him the first words exchanged in the story: "They have no wine." The repetition of information about the wine supply serves to highlight its importance, just as information about the severity of an illness emphasizes the significance of a miracle in healing accounts (e.g., 5:2–7, 9:1).

What is more difficult is understanding the force of the comment made by Jesus' mother. Does "They have no wine" constitute a request for a miracle, as some interpreters have assumed, or is it merely a device designed to prompt the saying of Jesus and the miracle that eventually follows? The statement taken on its own is no more than a report, neutral in its expectations. No miracle has preceded this event, so that the mother might know what to anticipate. Appeals to her special knowledge of her son's identity and abilities are out of order, since we are confining ourselves to the story as John's Gospel narrates it. Only when read in the context of Jesus' response in verse 4 do the words of his mother take on the coloration of a request for intervention, but the change between verse 3 and verse 4 is significant. The mother's initial words do no more than convey to Jesus the information the narrator has already supplied to the reader: there is no more wine for the feast. Unless we are to assume that the reader knows the conventional form of a miracle story and therefore expects a miracle to follow, we must conclude that the statement of Jesus' mother simply underscores the need for wine and brings that need to Jesus' attention. (Even a highly informed reader might miss the "clue" that a miracle will follow, given the fact that the "need" indicated here differs considerably from the situations that precipitate most miracle stories. There is no sick person, no lack of food, no boat tossed by a storm.)[6]

To this point, the story is straightforward. Even if the reader has come to suspect that a miracle will supply the missing wine, this story generates little tension. But when Jesus speaks in verse 4, tension does indeed make its entrance. Here every element in the statement raises questions, especially questions about how the mother of Jesus is to be understood—the question Jesus asks, the address of his mother as "Woman," and the pronouncement about his "hour." The ambiguities presented by Jesus' question and comment can be illustrated by surveying a few modern translations.

NRSV   "Woman, what concern is that to you and to me? My hour has not yet come."

RSV   "O woman, what have you to do with me? My hour has not yet come."

TEV   "You must not tell me what to do," Jesus replied. "My time has not yet come."

NAB   [And] Jesus said to her, "Woman, how does your concern affect me? My hour has not yet come."

REB   He answered, "That is no concern of mine. My hour has not yet come."

NJV   Jesus said, "Woman, what do you want from me? My hour has not come yet."

NIV   "Dear woman, why do you involve me?" Jesus replied. "My time has not yet come."

The second sentence of Jesus' response changes little from one translation to the next, but there is great variation in the treatment of the initial question. That variation stems in large part from the difficulty of the Greek question, *ti emoi kai soi, gynai,* which may be translated quite literally (and nearly unintelligibly) as: "What is to me and to you, woman?" Its equivalent appears in the synoptic Gospels in the words of demons who find their power threatened by the presence of Jesus (Mark 1:24, 5:7), but it probably comes into both the synoptic and the Johannine traditions from its usage in the Septuagint, where it appears in two different ways.

In some passages "What is to me and to you?" means something like "What do you have against me?" as when the widow of Zarephath accuses Elijah of causing the life-threatening illness of her son (1 Kgs 17:18) or when Jephthah asks why the Ammonite king has come to fight him (Judg 11:12; see also 2 Chr 35:21, 1 Esdr 1:26). In other passages the question serves to reject a request, as when David rebukes Abishai who wishes to kill one of David's enemies (2 Sam 16:10; see also 2 Sam 19:22, 2 Kgs 3:13). The difficulty with using these examples to unpack the meaning of Jesus' statement in John 2:4 is that in the examples the context makes the question's meaning clear—but the same does not hold true in John. The context here gives virtually no indication of what Jesus' words mean. Interpreters therefore inevitably employ their perception about the whole story in order to translate this verse.

Since it is difficult to imagine how the mother's words could be construed as hostile to Jesus, perhaps the former meaning is ruled out. The latter meaning, that of a request denied, thus gains in strength—but unclarity remains precisely about what the request might be and why it is rejected. While all of the translations cited above see in Jesus' words a denial of his mother's request, the force of that denial varies greatly from translation to translation. The NAB and REB read Jesus' response as a rejection of a concern that belongs to his mother, while the NRSV distances both Jesus and his mother from the need. This translation, while grammatically possible, seems unwarranted, since the question nowhere else has that connotation. The Good News Bible (TEV), with its "You must not tell me what to do," goes even further, paraphrasing Jesus' ambiguous question into a clear rejection of his mother's right to make a request of him.

Jesus' question rejects the "request" that is now revealed to be implicit in his mother's words, but the precise meaning of his rejection remains ambiguous, with the result of increasing the tension in the incident. Enhancing that tension is the form of address with which Jesus' rejection ends: "Woman." In contemporary English usage, addressing an individual as "Woman," as in "Woman, what time is it?" or "Woman, here is your ticket" (as distinct from "Excuse me, ma'am, can you tell me what time it is?" or "Here is your ticket, ma'am") seems abrupt, even rude. By no means, however, does the translation of *gynē* as "woman" imply the same rudeness or hostility on the part of Jesus. One difficulty we encounter in this verse, then, is that we have no English counterpart for the nuance of the Greek.

Elsewhere in John's Gospel, Jesus addresses other women in the same manner. When he speaks to the Samaritan woman, he says, "Woman, believe me, the hour is coming . . ." (John 4:21). His initial words to Mary Magdalene after the resurrection are, "Woman, why are you weeping?" (20:15; cf. 20:13). In the synoptic Gospels also, Jesus addresses women in the same way (see Matt 15:28, Luke 13:12). What makes this particular address in John 2:4 strange is that it applies to his own mother. Some interpreters see in this address a confirmation of the rejection implied in the preceding question, so that Jesus denies not only the request that may be implicit in his mother's statement but even her maternal relationship to him. She is not "mother," but [merely] "woman." The difficulty with this reading of Jesus' comment is twofold: (1) The narrator continues to associate Jesus with his mother, with no indication that this incident has severed or altered their relationship (2:12, 6:42, 19:25), and (2) the address "woman" nowhere else carries a hostile tone (see, e.g., 4:21, 20:15).

More prevalent among interpreters is the notion that "woman" invests Jesus' mother with a symbolic role. On this view, she represents some larger group in a significant theological way. While there are many variations of this viewpoint, Raymond Brown's analysis of Mary's role in this passage is significant, both because it synthesizes the earlier work of a number of scholars and because it has in turn exerted considerable influence. Brown connects this passage with Revelation 12, where a "woman" *(gynē)* gives birth to a male child, a messianic figure, who is snatched away from her and taken to heaven; a great dragon, unable to seize the child, battles against the woman and her other children. This woman is thought to symbolize the people of God, from whom (in the form of Israel) the Messiah is born and who (in the form of the church) persists in protecting her persecuted children. Brown sees in Gen 3:15 the background description of the woman in Revelation 12, and finds in both passages important connections with Jesus' mother in John: (1) All three texts (Gen 3:15, John 2:4, Revelation 12) feature a "woman"; John's usage would be understandable if Jesus' mother, like the other two women, is regarded in terms of the Eve of Genesis 3; (2) Revelation 12 clearly echoes Genesis 3, and the early chapters of John likewise echo the early chapters of Genesis; (3) As Revelation 12 refers to the other children of the woman, the disciples of Jesus appear in both Johannine texts in which his mother plays a part. Brown concludes from these associations that Jesus' refusal to act upon his mother's implicit request means that she has no role in his earthly ministry, which stems entirely from the will of the Father. However, she does receive a role when Jesus' "hour" comes; at the cross Jesus grants her the guardianship of the Beloved Disciple. Mary is thus, for Brown and others, "the New Eve, the symbol of the Church; the Church has no role during the ministry of Jesus but only after the hour of his resurrection and ascension."[7]

Later we shall return to the larger question whether Jesus' mother is a symbolic figure in John. At this point, the important issue is whether the analysis Brown offers illumines the usage of the term *woman* for Jesus' mother in 2:4. Although the word *woman (gynē)* appears in all three texts, the strange use of *woman* in direct address to a mother occurs only in John. If we are to think that its use in 2:4 makes Jesus' mother a symbolic figure, then why not draw the same conclusion concerning Jesus' address to the Samaritan woman and to Mary Magdalene? Are they also symbols of Eve or of the church?

The precise connotation of the address of Jesus' mother as "woman" remains unclear, and admitting that unclarity is preferable to forcing some preconceived notion on the text. Like the preceding question, "What is to me and to you?" it is ambiguous, perhaps even intentionally so. Whatever their *theological* connotation, both parts of Jesus' response serve to draw the reader's attention to what follows. The ambiguity is meaningful and moves the story forward. Because neither the question nor the address has a meaning that is immediately clear, readers are invited to look further, to give attention to what follows. In fact, the parallel addresses to the Samaritan woman ("Woman, believe me, the hour is coming when you will worship the Father neither on this mountain nor in Jerusalem," 4:21) and to Mary Magdalene ("Woman, why are you weeping? Whom are you looking for?" 20:15) work in the same way. The address calls for the reader's attention and underscores the statement that follows.

The NRSV, along with the NAB and the REB, translates the final portion of Jesus' response as, "My hour has not yet come," but a very literal translation, preserving the Greek word order, would be: "Not yet has come the hour my." Up to the final word of this statement, the expectation of the reader might be that Jesus is speaking of the right time for the wine or the right hour of the feast. Only with the final word, "my," is the "hour" revealed to be something entirely other than the right hour of the celebration at hand. Even then, the statement will remain unclear, since neither Jesus nor any other character has previously referred to "the hour." Only as the story progresses will the nature of Jesus' hour as the hour of his crucifixion be revealed (see, e.g., 12:23, 27; 13:1; 16:2; 17:1). One must have read or heard all of the Gospel to understand the early hints about the rejection of Jesus.[8]

What we have, then, in the exchange between Jesus and his mother becomes understandable only in retrospect. Her report about the lack of wine prompts a response that is extremely difficult to understand. By prefacing Jesus' puzzling statement about his hour with even more puzzling comments to his mother, John effectively causes the reader to wonder what is going on—especially what the hour is to which he refers. As other references appear, they will surely stand out in the reader's mind. When the "hour" does in fact come, this early story will be recalled.

That the statements of Jesus in verse 4 have their role in anticipation of the later "hour" but little role in the story at hand seems to find confirmation in the fact that the story proceeds with no reference to Jesus' statements. His mother's order to the waiters in verse 5 reflects nothing of what he has said. Her order may be said to acknowledge Jesus' authority, but it provides no indication of what she expects or why she gives the direction that she gives. The miracle story itself again proceeds and, within it, her role is primarily that of assisting in setting the stage for what follows.

Although the mother of Jesus disappears from view between her words to the waiters in verse 5 and the brief reference to her in verse 12, we need to attend to the remainder of the story in order to assess its meaning and importance and hence the mother's role within it. In verse 6 the story resumes, much as it began, with a report of who or what was there. As in verse 1, where we read that the "mother of Jesus was there," in verse 6 we learn that "six stone jars were there" (author's translation). The stage is now set. Commentators often and rightly point out that these six stone jars, each of which could contain fifteen to twenty-five gallons, signify the fantastic abundance of the gifts introduced by Christ. Whatever follows, it is to be a story of great extravagance. As Paul Meyer comments, the Cana story "is not primarily about a humble Galilean village wedding but about the Bringer of divine gifts."[9]

One unusual feature of the miracle that follows has to do with the way in which various characters know—and do not know—what is going on in the story. As his mother had done, Jesus addresses himself to the waiters and instructs them to fill these large jars with water. The narrator then tells us that the waiters filled them up to the top. Jesus then tells the same waiters to take some of this (presumed) water to the chief waiter. The narrator confirms that the waiters do as Jesus tells them. Only as the headwaiter drinks from the water do the readers learn that it had been turned into wine, and the headwaiter did not know it was transformed water—but of course, neither did the readers know it in a direct way! The waiters know where it came from, but it remains unclear that they know it is wine. Ironically, the headwaiter calls out to the bridegroom with the closing statement: "Everyone serves the good wine first, and then the inferior wine after the guests have become drunk. But you have kept the good wine until now."

The presence in this story of water, wine, and a wedding has led interpreters to dwell on its symbolism, identifying these and other specific features of the story with theological concepts outside the story. The importance of this story, however, goes well beyond these individual elements of symbolism, for this story also teases the imagination. Most of what is needed in order to understand the story is *not* said: What is the relationship between Jesus and his mother? What is the hour? When and how does the miracle occur? How are "inferior wine" and "good wine" to be understood? How do Jesus' disciples understand that this is a sign? What leads to their belief? The story teases the reader by offering bits and pieces of itself. Its function, from a literary standpoint, is not so much to narrate this particular event as to point forward. Jesus emerges here as the one who brings extravagant gifts to human beings, gifts of abundance almost beyond imagining, but the precise nature of those gifts remains to be explicated. The story also introduces Jesus' "hour" but leaves that important notion unexplained. What John presents here is a symbolic story, but it is also an anticipatory event.[10] Verse 11 marks the closing of the story with the notation that this was the first of Jesus' signs and that his disciples believed in him.[11] The narrator then comments that Jesus went to Capernaum "with his mother, his brothers, and his disciples; and they remained there a few days" (v. 12). As noted earlier, this association of Jesus with his mother contradicts the notion that at Cana he rejects her or repudiates his tie to his physical family. On the other hand, what does it mean that the narrator explains in verse 11 that "his disciples" believed in him but says nothing of the faith of his mother and brothers? Does their continued physical presence imply faith, or does the absence of a statement about their belief imply unbelief? The answers to these questions are unclear. What is clear is that Jesus has a physical, earthly family.

Before turning to the second Johannine scene in which Jesus' mother appears, it will be helpful to draw the threads together by stating concisely the role and function she has in the Cana scene. The history of the interpretation of this passage reveals a wide variety of interpretations of Mary. This diversity of viewpoints reflects not only the diversity of the interpreters but the unclarity of the story itself as well. The story, as we have seen, teems with symbolism, but its importance goes well beyond its symbolic or alle-gorical application. The story is proleptic; it anticipates the gifts of God that Jesus will bring, the hour of Jesus' revelation, and the need for decision about Jesus.

The function of the mother of Jesus within this story is both simple and profound. At one level she is merely a functionary, a part of setting the stage for the event. From a literary point of view, her words to Jesus and to the servants provoke the action of the miracle, but that is not to say that she knows a miracle is at hand or that she intends to provoke Jesus into a dra-matic action. Had some other woman, otherwise unknown to us, taken this part in the story, interpreters would hasten to emphasize the vast gulf be-tween that woman and Jesus.

A second way in which Jesus' mother functions within this story is to connect this first reference to Jesus' hour to the hour itself, namely, the hour of his crucifixion. Because she appears at only these two points in John's narrative, the reference to the hour here surely points ahead to her second appearance in chapter 19. Is this connection solely a literary device, or does some substantive connection exist between the mother and the hour? The answer to that question can only come with a closer examination of her appearance at the crucifixion scene.

A third function of Jesus' mother within this story, and one not gener-ally recognized, is to assert the humanity of Jesus. Reading the references to Jesus' mother in the context of earlier references to Jesus' home in Galilee (1:45–46), his father Joseph (1:45), and the later reference to his brothers (2:12) re-interprets who Jesus is. If the prologue, with its claim that Jesus is "word" and "light," "grace" and "truth," creates the impression that Jesus has only a kind of docetic existence, one that appears to be but is not really human, then the end of chapter 1 and the beginning of chapter 2 correct that impression. If, as is sometimes said, the Cana miracle separates Jesus from his mother, it is also true that the Cana miracle and the passage that precedes it *invest* Jesus with a human mother and father and brothers and home. Here the narrator portrays dramatically the words of 1:14: "And the Word became flesh and lived among us."

"STANDING NEAR THE CROSS" (JOHN 19:25–27)

The mother of Jesus returns to John's narrative only in a very brief and puzzling scene at Jesus' crucifixion.[12] John's account of the crucifixion itself consists of four episodes: the actual crucifixion and the inscription Pilate orders placed upon the cross (19:16b–22), the division of Jesus' clothing among the soldiers (19:23–25a), the words of Jesus to his mother and Beloved Disciple (19:25b–27), and Jesus' death (19:28–30). In the third of these episodes and without a word of preparation, the narrator introduces Jesus' mother along with three other women. Apart from her appellation, "his mother," not a single word describes her. She utters not so much as a syllable. The only action she takes is that of "standing near the cross."

Despite this meager presentation, or perhaps because of it, interpreters have stridently debated the significance of Mary's presence at the cross. Some scholars, including the majority of Protestant interpreters, view this scene as having primarily emotional rather than theological importance. Ernst Haenchen contrasts this scene with Mark's portrait of Jesus' isolation at his crucifixion and notes that the Johannine Jesus "savours the proximity of those close to him." [13] On this reading, Jesus' words to the Beloved Disciple and to his mother are simply an indication of filial piety. He is unwilling to die without securing care and protection for his mother.

Other scholars see in this episode at the cross, as in the wedding at Cana, a significant event in which Jesus' mother plays a highly symbolic role. Suggestions about the nature of that symbolism vary widely. Some argue that the relationship depicted here between Jesus' mother and the Beloved Disciple symbolizes the unity of the church, with Mary becoming the mother of the faithful and the Beloved Disciple the ideal convert. [14] Others see in her presence a symbol of Jewish Christianity, with the Beloved Disciple representing the Gentile Christianity that is obliged to honor Jewish Christianity as its own mother. [15] In keeping with one ancient strand of interpretation, another approach understands the mother of Jesus here as symbolic of the church. Having been denied a role at Cana, during the ministry of Jesus, she now emerges at Jesus' hour to "bring forth Christian children in the image of her son." [16]

A reassessment of this debate requires a careful re-reading of the text. Before turning to that task, however, one issue that needs to be addressed is the fact that the narrator never refers to Jesus' mother by her proper name. Although we have already encountered this practice in the Cana scene, it becomes especially acute in John 19 since Mary appears together with the important and also unnamed figure of the Beloved Disciple. The connection between the two figures has led some to conclude that John uses unnamed characters as representative or symbolic figures. [17]

The difficulty with such an attractive generalization, however, is that it falls victim to the evidence of the text. If anyone is symbolic in John's Gospel, surely it must be the named character Nicodemus, who represents those who want to confess their faith in Jesus, but safely, in the dark. Similarly Pilate may be said to represent all those who cannot come to a decision about Jesus. The correlation between named and unrepresentative, unnamed and representative, simply does not hold. Moreover, in the case of Jesus' mother, the fact that she is not named can be accounted for in other ways. Perhaps John refers to her as he does because he sees her importance simply in the fact of her relationship to Jesus. Perhaps he does not know her name. If Jesus' mother is a symbolic character in this incident, her symbolism needs to emerge from the story itself rather than from the mere fact that she is not named.

Indeed, the question of whether this episode is a symbolic episode or an emotional one probably constitutes a false dichotomy. Both answers are right, if we are asking about the experience of the reader. If a character is symbolic because readers identify with that character, then it is undeniable that for some readers the mother of Jesus is symbolic. It is equally undeniable that many readers will find this scene at the cross to be an emotional one. The question is whether the passage can be read in some other way, apart from either of these interpretations. I contend that it can, and that the primary function of this scene is to complete the crucifixion's separation of Jesus from all that belongs to his earthly life. Just as he is stripped of his clothing, he divests himself of his mother and his Beloved Disciple. The human family that is ascribed to him early in the Gospel, and especially at Cana, here is removed at the "hour" of his return to the Father. The issue is not that Jesus' mother is symbolic or representative, but that the scene as a whole symbolizes the culmination of Jesus' return to his Father.

In order to see how this reading of the passage is possible, we need first to examine this incident in relationship to the one that precedes it (19:23–24). Because the soldiers' actions toward Jesus are hostile, taking away Jesus' clothes and talking to one another about their disposition, while the women who stand "near the cross" are clearly allied with Jesus, the first thing we note is the contrast between the two groups. That contrast is reenforced by further contrasts. In the first scene, the characters are male, in the second female; in the first the characters are Romans and outsiders, in the second they are from among Jesus' own inner circle.

As strikingly different as the two stories are, they also stand together. Verse 25, which bridges the two scenes, may be translated somewhat literally as follows: "Therefore, on the one hand, the soldiers did these things, but, on the other hand, there stood near the cross of Jesus his mother and the sister of his mother, Mary the wife of Clopas, and Mary Magdalene" (author's translation).[18] By means of the phrases "on the one hand" and "on the other hand" (*men* and *de*), the narrator forges a tie between the two groups or the two incidents (as is also the case when the same Greek words appear elsewhere in the Gospel, as at 10:41; 16:9–10, 22; 20:30–31). The soldiers make four parts of Jesus' garments, so that each soldier receives a part. Counterbalancing this careful numerical note appear the four women in verse 25.[19] As contradictory as the two groups are, these scenes belong together within the narrative and must be understood in light of each other.

I shall return to the relationship between these two scenes after looking more closely at the remainder of verses 25–27. Before leaving the scene in which the soldiers divide Jesus' garments, however, the scriptural quotation in verse 24 warrants attention. There the narrator interprets the dividing of Jesus' clothes as a fulfillment of Ps 22:18:

> they divide my clothes among themselves,
> and for my clothing they cast lots.[20]

The scenes that follow verses 25–27 also refer to the fulfillment of scripture (see vv. 28, 36–37), prompting the question of whether our scene likewise carries some reference to scripture. Certainly the narrator makes no overt reference to scripture, as in the other scenes, but is there some more subtle allusion? Because of the connections between verses 23–24 and verses 25–27, Psalm 22 offers itself for consideration, particularly because of its obvious importance for early Christian interpretations of Jesus' death. Verses 9–11 of that psalm refer to the birth of the psalmist:

> Yet it was you who took me from the womb;
> you kept me safe on my mother's breast.
> On you I was cast from my birth,
> and since my mother bore me you have been my God.
> Do not be far from me,
> for trouble is near and there is no one to help.

Here the mother serves as a metonym for human life, in that God brings the psalmist safely to life and sustains life itself. God has been near, and God's presence is needed once again in a time of trouble. Certainly any connection between this passage and John 19:25–27 is conjectural, but perhaps the narrator sees Jesus' mother also as his connection with human, physical life.

Accompanying Jesus' mother are three other women: her sister, Mary the wife of Clopas, and Mary Magdalene.[21] Neither the sister nor Mary the wife of Clopas appears elsewhere in John's Gospel. Mary Magdalene, who figures prominently in the resurrection account in chapter 20, makes her first appearance here. Of these four characters, two are named and two unnamed. The two who are unnamed are not only relatives of each other but also of Jesus. The two named characters have no such family relationship. This pattern underscores the earlier suggestion that the author leaves Jesus' mother unnamed because what he understands as important about her is contained in this designation: she is Jesus' mother and, as such, she connects him with human life.

The narrator reveals nothing of the history or motivation of these four characters. Their single action is that they are "standing near the cross of Jesus." As observed earlier, this action already places them in opposition to the four soldiers, who are not "standing near" but over against. By contrast also with Judas, who stands with those who arrest Jesus (18:5), and with Peter, who stands "outside at the gate" while the high priest interrogates Jesus (18:16, cf. 18:18, 25), these women place themselves alongside as witnesses of Jesus' death.[22] One of them, Mary Magdalene, will later become a witness to the resurrection as she stands at Jesus' tomb (20:11).

Having introduced the four women, the narrator again turns attention to Jesus. First he sees and then he speaks, both actions so briefly described as to raise a multitude of questions. Of the four women who are present, the narrator refers only to Jesus' mother as being observed by him. And verse 26 reveals that the four women are not alone, as the Beloved Disciple is "standing beside her [the mother of Jesus]."[23]

John consistently associates the figure of the Beloved Disciple with the narrative of Jesus' death and resurrection. He first appears in the Gospel when he reclines next to Jesus at the meal that marks the beginning of the passion narrative (13:23–25). Almost certainly he is the unnamed disciple who follows Jesus into the high priest's courtyard, while Peter remains outside (18:15). Of the disciples, only this one stands at the cross. The resurrection narrative begins with his race against Peter to reach the tomb after Mary Magdalene tells them that the stone has been rolled away. The Gospel concludes with a reference to his role as witness of Jesus and purveyor of gospel tradition. The presence of the Beloved Disciple seems to mark every turning point in this second half of the Gospel.

When Jesus first speaks, however, he addresses his mother rather than the Beloved Disciple. As at the wedding in Cana, he addresses her as "Woman." The use of the same form of address for Jesus' mother recalls the earlier scene in which she appears and its reference to the "hour" to come.

The final words Jesus speaks to his mother are "Behold your son" (author's translation). Who is this "son" to whom Jesus refers? Until the following verse, with its parallel command to the Beloved Disciple, that question remains unanswered. The most natural conclusion would be that Jesus refers to himself, asking his mother to look once more upon her own child. Only with verse 27 does the narrator make it clear that the son to be looked upon is now the Beloved Disciple rather than Jesus. Jesus transfers that title from himself to his disciple by virtue of this direction.

The very fact that Jesus speaks first to his mother and only then to the Beloved Disciple suggests that this scene concerns something other than—

and more than—an act of filial piety.[24] Had the narrator wished simply to demonstrate that Jesus continued to exercise a child's obligation to care for his mother, he could have given only one instruction and that to the Beloved Disciple.

The two exhortations, "Behold your son," and "Behold your mother," have a number of counterparts earlier in the Gospel:

> 1:29   "Behold the lamb of God who takes away the sin of the world" (see also 1:36).
>
> 3:26   "Behold, this one baptizes and everyone comes to him."
>
> 19:14   "Behold your king."
>
> (author's translations)

The use of "Behold," here, as often in biblical narrative, signals that an important or unusual event is at hand.

The final sentence in this verse serves several purposes. By interrupting both the time of the narration ("from that hour") and its location ("into his own home"), the narrator hints at the continued existence of these two people who are closely related to Jesus. The specific response of the Beloved Disciple indicates that he will be obedient to the new relationship inaugurated by Jesus. This action also distances the mother and the Beloved Disciple from Jesus. No longer do they stand "near the cross." Even if we are not to imagine that the Beloved Disciple and Jesus' mother immediately left the scene after hearing Jesus' words, from the narrator's point of view they are gone. The Beloved Disciple reappears in chapters 20 and 21, but Jesus' mother does not. From this point on in John's story, Jesus has no mother.

Verse 28 reinforces the isolation that now envelops Jesus. Neither the Beloved Disciple, Jesus' mother, the other women, nor any other sympathetic individual stands by. The narrator explains that "after this" Jesus knew that everything was finished. He states his thirst in order to fulfill scripture, but the statement is made to no one in particular, and no one speaks to him. He drinks the wine that is offered and pronounces his own death.

These three brief scenes (vv. 23–25a, 25b–27, 28–30) stand closely connected, as we have observed. The four soldiers have in the four women their counterpart, and grammatically, as we have noted, the phrases "on the one hand" and "on the other" also connect these first two scenes. The third scene, that of the death itself, refers back to the preceding one with the introductory words "after this." By connecting together these three brief scenes, the narrator depicts the separation of Jesus from his earthly existence. First, he is stripped of his clothing by persons who are indifferent or even hostile to him. Second, he separates himself from those who stand close to him, even his mother and the disciple whom he loves.[25] Third, he takes a final drink of wine and gives up his own breath.

When we ask how this scene characterizes the mother of Jesus, the answer must be given in two different ways. As noted at the outset of this discussion, the narrator devotes not a single word to her description (apart from the appellation "his mother") and ascribes not a single word to her. Her sole action is to stand near the cross. Jesus addresses her only briefly. There is, in one sense, no "characterization" of Jesus' mother.

On the other hand, her presence at the cross recalls the only other occasion on which she was present and the initial announcement about Jesus' "hour." It also recalls the network of family that connects Jesus to earthly existence. When she and the Beloved Disciple are given to one another and depart the scene, Jesus' connections to earthly existence likewise depart from John's Gospel. Her role in this incident, then, has to do with Jesus' separation from his own earthly life.

This reading of the reference to Jesus' mother at the cross differs significantly from both of the dominant interpretations of this text. To see this incident, as many Protestant interpreters have, as a touching scene in which Jesus demonstrates his filial piety, is to read into the text issues that are strikingly absent. It is strange to suggest that Jesus demonstrates his devotion to his mother, when his first words call upon her to look upon her (new) "son," the Beloved Disciple. More important, the utter absence of emotion in the narrator's description of the incident argues against this interpretation. Nowhere in John does Jesus, who does weep for Lazarus and his sisters, and who later appears to a weeping Mary Magdalene, express emotional attachment to or concern for his mother.

The interpretations that see in Jesus' mother a symbol for some larger group likewise seem to overinterpret the passage. Despite the narrator's note about the future at the end of verse 27, the focus here is not on what happens to the Beloved Disciple and Jesus' mother but on the death of Jesus and, specifically, the separation of Jesus from those relationships that characterized his earthly existence. No longer the son of this woman, he may depart to be with his heavenly Father. In other words, as we saw in the Cana scene, the symbolism inheres in the scene as a whole rather than in some quasi-allegorical interpretation of the characters.

CONCLUSION

Before pulling together observations about the characterization of Mary in the Gospel of John, we need to look again at the two brief scenes in which she appears and the relationship between them. "Cana" and "The

Cross" do belong together, as the web of connections suggests: the presence of Jesus' mother at these and only these points in the narrative, the anticipation (in chapter 2) and culmination (in chapter 19) of Jesus' "hour," and the references to wine, first the wine of the wedding and then the wine given to Jesus on the cross.[26]

Two important motifs emerge from the close connection between these two events. First, Jesus, the bearer of unimaginably great gifts to human beings as proleptically announced in the gift of an amazing quantity of wine, ultimately gives himself. The notion that Jesus' death constitutes a loving gift, of course, appears earlier in the Gospel (10:11–18, 15:13), but here the narrator depicts it most graphically. Second, the first scene and its context invest Jesus with a human family from which he must separate at the cross. Jesus, who is the Logos of God, also has a human father, a mother, and brothers, as the wedding at Cana demonstrates. His return to the heavenly Father, however, requires separation from this human family, just as it requires the giving up of his life. An interesting tension emerges in the contrast between the two episodes. In 2:1–11, Jesus is invested with a human family, yet retains some distance from that family; in 19:25b–27, Jesus completes his removal from the earthly sphere but, in so doing, he cements a familial relationship among those "near the cross" whom he leaves behind.

The Role of Mary

Mary's role in the Gospel of John consists exclusively of her relationship to Jesus. She remains unnamed because what makes her important is nothing other than the fact that she is Jesus' mother. While this might be said of the treatment of Mary in Luke and Matthew as well, Luke does portray her as an individual who can interpret the events around her and who responds to them in her own way. Although Matthew depicts Mary exclusively as mother, he does understand that she is threatened by the actions Joseph contemplates as she is by Herod's plots against her child. John's references to "the mother of Jesus" leave little room for her to interpret or even to be threatened. She exists in the narrative to reveal something about Jesus, not something about herself.

This observation may prompt the charge that John's Gospel thereby slights this signficant female, and certainly modern readers would wish to know more about Mary. That desire need not give rise to a rebuke of an author whose concerns are quite different from our own, however. If John treats Mary as significant only by virtue of her relationship to Jesus, he treats other characters no differently. One reason scholars have found the figure of the Beloved Disciple so elusive is that John describes him only in relationship to Jesus. No other information helps the reader to identify the Beloved Disciple, because he is important for the narrator only by virtue of his closeness to Jesus. Mary receives the same treatment male characters do, because John's is a story solely about Jesus.

Mary and Narrative Development

As our examination of the relevant scenes has demonstrated, John limits Mary's role within the developing narrative. It is her comment that provokes the first reference by Jesus to his "hour," and her reappearance at that "hour" ties the end of the Gospel back to its beginning. Her presence on both occasions allows John first to depict Jesus' earthly connectedness and then to demonstrate his separation from that connectedness. In neither aspect of this narrative development is Mary essential. Another character might have underscored the first references to the "hour" and the "hour" itself, just as Jesus' brothers might have been substituted for Mary at the cross. For John, she serves a convenient but not a necessary function.

Mary and the "Order" of John

With a story as rich and mysterious as that of the Fourth Gospel, any attempt to state its overarching "order" will prove frustrating. Perhaps the best identification of the "order" of this narrative comes from the text itself. In 1:14 the narrator proclaims that "the Word became flesh and lived among us, and we have seen his glory, the glory as of a father's only son, full of grace and truth." This statement captures both the glory that John ascribes to Jesus and the "en-fleshment" of that glory in a human being. The narrative scarcely maintains a balance between these two poles, however, for over and over Jesus' unity with God eclipses his humanity.[27] Given this "order" to the story John tells, the minimal role ascribed to Mary becomes understandable. Her role is tied to indications of Jesus' humanity—his earthly family and his death. She serves to ensure the humanity of Jesus, but that humanity inevitably plays a subsidiary role in this gospel of glory.

NOTES

1. As with Matthew and Luke, I refer to the author of the Fourth Gospel as John primarily as a convenience. I am not assuming that the author is to be identified with any particular historical figure.

2. For a careful discussion of this debate, see D. Moody Smith, *John Among the Gospels: The Relationship in Twentieth-Century Research* (Minneapolis: Fortress, 1992).

3. For a discussion of some earlier critics' embarrassment over this miracle, see Martin Hengel, "The Interpretation of the Wine Miracle at Cana: John 2:1–11," in *The Glory of Christ in the New Testament: Studies in Christology in Memory of George Bradford Caird*, ed. L. D. Hurst and N. T. Wright (Oxford: Clarendon Press, 1987) 83–90.

4. John 1:14 stands at the center of a complex debate about the nature of Johannine christology. I am not here entering into that debate but only noting that this verse contains the single indication that the Logos is or becomes a human being. For a helpful discussion of the debate, see Marianne Meye Thompson, *The Humanity of Jesus in the Fourth Gospel* (Philadelphia: Fortress, 1988).

5. See Thompson, *Humanity of Jesus,* 25: "That Jesus is from heaven does not necessarily imply that he is not also 'the son of Joseph.' "

6. Contrast the judgment of Jeffrey Lloyd Staley, who argues that by the end of verse 3, "the implied author has already aroused the implied reader's expectations for a miraculous event" (*The Print's First Kiss: A Rhetorical Investigation of the Implied Reader in the Fourth Gospel* [SBLDS 82; Atlanta: Scholars, 1988] 83).

7. Raymond E. Brown, *The Gospel According to John* (AB 29; 2 vols.; Garden City: Doubleday, 1966, 1970) 1:108–9.

8. Wayne A. Meeks's observation about John's Gospel is pertinent: "The reader cannot understand any part of the Fourth Gospel until he understands the whole. The reader has an experience rather like that of the dialogue partners of Jesus: either he will find the whole business so convoluted, obscure, and maddeningly arrogant that he will reject it in anger, or he will find it so fascinating that he will stick with it until the progressive reiteration of themes brings, on some level of consciousness at least, a degree of clarity" ("The Man from Heaven in Johannine Sectarianism," *JBL* 91 [1972] 68–69).

9. Paul W. Meyer, "John 2:10," *JBL* 86 (1967) 193.

10. "The symbolism of the story is general and difficult to pin down, but it is characteristic of the evangelist to explicate his own earlier passages in the course of the book itself" (Meyer, "John 2:10," 107). Similarly, Hengel refers to this miracle as programmatic for the whole of the Gospel and contends that it is to be interpreted in a variety of ways "so that it can be related to the whole Gospel through a 'dense and coherent'. . . web of references" ("The Interpretation of the Wine Miracle at Cana," 102).

11. Verse 11 also specifies again that Cana is in Galilee (see 2:1), a region that is associated with acceptance of Jesus in John's Gospel. See Wayne A. Meeks, "Galilee and Judea in the Fourth Gospel," *JBL* 85 (1966) 159–69, and the modifications of Jouette M. Bassler, "The Galileans: A Neglected Factor in Johannine Community Research," *CBQ* 43 (1981) 243–57.

12. There is, in addition, in John 6:42 a brief reference to the fact that people know Jesus' parents ("They were saying, 'Is not this Jesus, the son of Joseph, whose father and mother we know?' ").

13. Ernst Haenchen, *John 2: A Commentary on the Gospel of John Chapters 7–21,* trans. Robert W. Funk (Hermeneia; Philadelphia: Fortress, 1984) 193.

14. E. C. Hoskyns, *The Fourth Gospel* (London: Faber and Faber, 1947) 530.

15. Rudolf Bultmann, *The Gospel of John* (Philadelphia: Westminster, 1971) 672.

16. Raymond E. Brown, *John,* 2:923–27. Brown also sees in the mother of Jesus themes connected with the figure of Lady Zion and with Eve. In his more recent work, however, Brown modifies this position; the scene demonstrates symbolically "how one related to Jesus by the flesh (his mother who is part of his natural family) becomes related to him by the Spirit (a member of the ideal discipleship)" (*The Death of the Messiah: From Gethsemane to the Grave* [2 vols.; New York: Doubleday, 1994] 2:1024).

17. Paul S. Minear, "The Beloved Disciple in the Gospel of John: Some Clues and Conjectures," *NovT* 19 (1977) 105–106; Margaret Pamment, "The Fourth Gospel's Beloved Disciple," *ExpTim* 94 (1983) 363–67. David Beck has argued that the unnamed characters in John serve as models of discipleship, pulling the reader into the story, but he is surely overinterpreting the Cana story to see in the mother of Jesus "a response of faith" ("The Narrative Function of Anonymity in Fourth Gospel Characterization," *Semeia* 63 [1993] 150).

18. The Greek text begins verse 25 only with the reference to the women, but the NRSV begins verse 25 with the final comment about the soldiers. In both cases the divisions between verses are, of course, entirely artificial.

19. Hoskyns, *The Fourth Gospel,* 530; Michel de Goedt, "Un schème de révélation dans le Quatrième Évangile," *NTS* 8 (1962) 142–50.

20. Ps 22:19 in the Hebrew.

21. Grammatically, it is possible that there are only three women in all: the mother of Jesus, her sister *who is* Mary the wife of Clopas, and Mary Magdalene. If Jesus' mother was actually named Mary, however, then it is highly unlikely that her sister also bore the name of Mary.

22. Barnabas Lindars also identifies the women as witnesses (*The Gospel of John* [NCB; London: Oliphants, 1972] 579).

23. The absence of the Beloved Disciple in verse 25 underscores the opposition between the four women of verse 25 and the four men in the preceding scene.

24. So also Raymond Collins, "Mary in the Fourth Gospel. A Decade of Johannine Studies," *Louvain Studies* 3 (1970) 99–142.

25. Henri van den Bussche sees this scene as enacting Jesus' abandonment by men and fulfilling Ps 69:8: "I have become a stranger to my kindred, an alien to my mother's children" (*Jean: Commentaire de l'évangel spirituel* [Bible et Vie Chrétienne; Bruges: Desclée de Brouwer, 1967] 527-29; cited in Collins, "Mary in the Fourth Gospel," 136).

26. Note, however, that the Greek word that refers to wine in John 2:1–12 *(oinos)* differs from that in 19:29–30 *(oxos).*

27. D. Moody Smith, *John* (Proclamation Commentaries; 2nd ed.; Philadelphia: Fortress, 1986) 66.

CHAPTER 5

A Life of Sacred Purity

Mary in the Protevangelium of James

My flesh is at a distance from me.
Yet approach and touch it:
It is as near as anyone can come.
　　Laura Riding, "The Virgin"

The New Testament offers only fleeting glimpses of Mary, as the preceding chapters have demonstrated. Most New Testament documents do not
mention her at all. Others simply refer to the fact that Jesus was "born of
woman" (e.g., Gal 4:4) or relate an incident involving Jesus' family (e.g.,
Mark 6:3). Where she does appear in Matthew, Luke, and John, her role is
a minor one. As is the case with other characters in the Gospels, Mary
enters the story strictly because her presence serves some larger point being
made about Jesus. To put it succinctly, the New Testament exhibits no interest in Mary as such, but only in Mary as a character in the story of Jesus.

We find the first evidence of Christian interest in Mary herself in the
second-century narrative the Protevangelium of James. The Protevangelium
is very much an anomaly, however, because the non-canonical Christian
writings of the late first century and the second century demonstrate little
interest in Mary. No reference to Mary appears in such early Christian writings as *Barnabas, 1 Clement*, the *Didache*, the *Epistle to Diognetus,*
Hermas, Papias, or the *Epistle of Polycarp*. Most of the apocryphal and
gnostic texts from this period make brief, if any, references to Mary. When
she does enter the discussion, it is almost entirely in connection with contro-
versies that are more aptly described as christological than as mariological.

This chapter will briefly survey the debates of the second century that
touch on what would later be called "Marian themes" and then will turn to
a close examination of the Protevangelium of James. The initial survey is
intended to provide a background against which to understand the distinctive
concerns of the Protevangelium. The chapter as a whole will expose ways
in which second-century Christianity duplicates some of the concerns regard-

ing Mary that are evident already in the New Testament and also develops new lines in the treatment of Mary. Sustained attention to the Protevangelium in particular has the advantage of allowing us to see an additional narrative presentation of Mary and to observe what happens when a narrative becomes interested in Mary for her own sake.

MARY IN SECOND-CENTURY CHRISTIANITY

E. R. Dodds once observed that "there are no periods in history; only in historians."[1] Dodds's wisdom reminds us that limiting this examination to writings of the second century is patently artificial. Other surveys of Mary in the patristic period are readily available, however, and the goal of this venture beyond the canon is not to duplicate or supplant those studies but to give attention to one important narrative that does concern Mary and to place that narrative in some comprehensible framework.[2]

Of the issues regarding Mary that concern the writers of the patristic period, four appear already in the second century, although in greatly differing degrees: Mary's maternity, her virginity, her sinlessness, and her function as the Second Eve.[3]

The Maternity of Mary

Recalling the christological nature of the controversy over Mary's maternity, this issue might better be referred to as the "sonship of Jesus." What is at stake here is whether and how Mary can rightfully be said to be Jesus' mother. On the one hand, for the docetists, who regarded Jesus as bearing only the appearance of a human being without actually becoming one, Mary was nothing other than a vessel through whom Jesus passed. For some gnostics, on the other hand, the human child born to Mary could not possibly be Son of God. He only became Son of God later when God adopted him. In order to counter these teachings, other Christians argued along two lines: (1) Jesus was in fact born of the woman Mary, and (2) the very same Jesus who was born to Mary is God.[4]

As early as the letters of Ignatius (ca. 110–115 C.E.), we find rejection of the docetic contention that Jesus did not really suffer and, along with that, the assertion that Jesus was "truly born" (alēthōs egennēthē) of Mary (The Trallians 9.1; ANF 1:60).

In his lengthy reply to the Valentinians' notion that Jesus merely "passed through" Mary, Irenaeus (around 180 C.E.) reviewed the evidence of the Gospels, especially emphasizing the Lukan account in which Jesus is acknowledged as Savior even in his mother's womb and as a babe in his mother's arms. Irenaeus interprets Simeon's canticle to mean that Simeon knows that "Jesus, born of Mary, was Christ Himself, the Son of God, the light of all, the glory of Israel itself" (*Against Heresies* 3.16.4; *ANF* 1:441). Elsewhere Irenaeus insists that the typology of Christ as the second Adam (see Romans 5 and 1 Corinthians 15) fails if Christ was not a real human being, if Christ "took nothing from the Virgin" while in her womb (*Against Heresies* 3.22.1; *ANF* 1:454).

Irenaeus looks to the broad sweep of the New Testament for confirmation that Jesus was born of a woman; by contrast, Tertullian (early third century) ingeniously constructs his argument for Mary's maternity from minor details in the Gospel narratives. When Jesus' mother and brothers come to find him, Jesus responds that those who actually hear and obey God are his mothers and brothers (see Matt 12:46–50; Mark 3:31–35; Luke 8:19–21); however, Tertullian insists, Jesus does not *deny* Mary's physical maternity. More important, Jesus could scarcely have transferred the blessedness of his mother to his disciples without implicitly acknowledging that Mary was his mother (*Against Marcion* 4.26.13; *ANF* 3:393; see also *On the Flesh of Christ* 7.79–81; *ANF* 3:529).

The Virginity of Mary

The canonical Gospels' claims regarding the virginity of Mary inevitably gave rise to controversy between Christians and non-Christians. These debates, at least as we reconstruct them from Christian sources, centered not, as might be imagined, on the Gospel accounts but on the correct interpretation of Isa 7:14: "Therefore the Lord himself will give you a sign. Look, the young woman is with child and shall bear a son, and shall name him Immanuel."

Justin (martyred around 165 C.E.) anticipates that the Gospel stories will be understood, along the lines of Greek and Roman mythology, as implying that God descended to earth and had intercourse with a woman. He appeals to Isa 7:14, which he takes to mean that "a virgin should conceive without intercourse. For if she had had intercourse with any one whatever, she was no longer a virgin" (*First Apology* 33.4; *ANF* 1:174).

Justin also responds to Jewish charges that Christians were mistranslating and misinterpreting Isa 7:14 (*Dialogue with Trypho* 67; *ANF* 1:231), but Irenaeus develops the response more fully. The well-known difficulty is that the Hebrew reads ʿalmāh or "young woman," while the Septuagint reads *parthenos*, "virgin." The Greek wording appears in Matt 1:23 and becomes crucial for Christian argumentation.[5] Irenaeus insists that Jews may not dismiss the Septuagint, since it was their own work and presumably represents their views (*Against Heresies* 3.21.1; *ANF* 1:451). Further, he notes that the Isaiah text introduces the statement about a "virgin" giving birth with the promise of a sign, which anticipates an "unlooked-for thing": "For what great thing or what sign should have been in this, that a young woman conceiving by a man should bring forth,—a thing which happens to all women that produce offspring? But since an unlooked-for salvation was to be provided for men through the help of God, so also was the unlooked-for birth from a virgin accomplished; God giving this sign, but man not working it out" (*Against Heresies* 3.21.6; *ANF* 1:453).[6]

Not all controversy regarding Mary's virginity addressed the matter of its facticity. Another question that arose concerned the exact nature of Mary's virginity. Was she a virgin when Jesus was conceived (virginity *ante partum*)? Did she remain a virgin even when Jesus was born, as the Protevangelium clearly maintains (virginity *in partu*)? Did she remain a virgin both prior to conception, during birth, and thereafter as well (virginity *post partum*)? This matter becomes quite controverted later on, but in the early centuries the only clear reference to the virginity *in partu* (apart from what we shall see in the Protevangelium) occurs in Clement of Alexandria, who reports that "many even down to our own time regard Mary, on account of the birth of her child, as having been in the puerperal state, although she was not. For some say that, after she brought forth, she was found, when examined, to be a virgin" (*Stromata* 7:16; *ANF* 2:551).[7] Tertullian may have this same tradition in mind when he asserts that Mary "ought rather to be called not a virgin than a virgin, becoming a mother at a leap, as it were, before she was a wife" (*On the Flesh of Christ* 23; *ANF* 3:541).

The Sinlessness of Mary

In keeping with the general observation that discussions of Mary in the second century are subsidiary to debates about Jesus, the issue of Mary's sinlessness receives only incidental attention. Irenaeus, while discussing the perfection and completion of Jesus, praises his awareness of the appropriate time and order for events. When Mary urged him to undertake "the wonderful miracle of the wine," Jesus, "checking her untimely haste," rebuked her (*Against Heresies* 3.16.7; *ANF* 1:443). In the course of Tertullian's argument that Mary must have been truly Jesus' mother or he would have denied having a mother when she and his brothers came to see him, Tertullian faults Mary and the brothers for their lack of faith at that time. He compares Mary with Israel, which stands outside the church while Christ is within (*On the Flesh of Christ* 7; *ANF* 3:527–29).

These few passages touching on the question of Mary's sinlessness assume that she was capable of error and apparently see no particular scandal in that assessment. The New Testament passages that come into the discussion are those that might be construed as casting a negative light on Mary. The Protevangelium's stress on the purity of Mary will contrast sharply with these passages. Since the Protevangelium does not present Jesus' ministry, however, it becomes difficult to compare that portrait with the assumption of Irenaeus and Tertullian that Mary was capable of error.

Mary as the Second Eve

The New Testament does not identify Mary as the second Eve, nor is she so characterized in the Protevangelium of James. Because the Eve-Mary typology plays a significant role in later discussions of Mary, however, it does warrant brief attention. The earliest comparison of Mary with Eve appears to be that of Justin, who briefly contrasts the two women. Eve, "who was a virgin and undefiled, having conceived the word of the serpent, brought forth disobedience and death." Mary, on the other hand, "received faith and joy, when the angel Gabriel announced the good tidings to her. . . . And by her has He been born, to whom we have proved so many Scriptures refer" (*Dialogue with Trypho* 100; *ANF* 1:249).

Irenaeus further develops this line of thought in the context of his discussion of Jesus as the second Adam. Mary's consent in Luke 1:38 demonstrates her obedience, which contrasts with Eve's disobedience. Like Justin, Irenaeus argues that Eve remained a virgin, despite her marriage to Adam; he explains that Eve and Adam were not yet adults and did not understand the process of procreation. Despite this fact, Eve disobeyed and became "the cause of death, both to herself and to the entire human race." By her obedience, however, Mary became "the cause of salvation, both to herself and the whole human race" (*Against Heresies* 3.22.4; *ANF* 1:455). Like Irenaeus, Tertullian understands Eve to be a virgin, who disobeys and gives birth to a kind of fratricidal devil, while Mary obeys and gives birth to a savior (*On the Flesh of Christ* 17; *ANF* 3:536).

This brief survey confirms the observation that interest in Mary in this period continues to be almost entirely derivative of christological questions: Can Jesus, the eternal Logos, Son of God, actually have been born of a woman? Is it possible that he was indeed born of a virgin? What work does he accomplish (i.e., the comparison between Jesus and Adam and therefore between Mary and Eve)? In the apocryphal and gnostic texts, as well as in the writings that would come to be regarded as orthodox, Mary occupies little attention. The one exception to that statement is the Protevangelium of James.

Because the Protevangelium is often identified as "popular" literature, it is sometimes dismissed as inappropriate for comparison with the more precise theological reflection of a Justin or an Irenaeus. Certainly the Protevangelium differs significantly from the early patristic writings, the most obvious difference being its genre. Justin and Irenaeus write treatises. The author of the Protevangelium, like the earlier evangelists, chooses the narrative form. And the author of the Protevangelium includes elements of legend, even of fancy. The early patristic writers are by no means devoid of interest in legend, however. More important, a sharp distinction between popular literature and that of the patristic writers seems inappropriate, especially so if the distinction results in a refusal to take the Protevangelium seriously as evidence of early Christian reflection on the mother of Jesus.

THE PROTEVANGELIUM OF JAMES

Ironically, although the Protevangelium of James has exerted enormous influence on Christian understandings of Mary, the narrative itself is today largely unknown outside scholarly circles.[8] From the Protevangelium are derived a number of the most treasured traditions about Mary, including the names of her parents (Joachim and Anna), the picture of Joseph as an elderly widower, the birth of Jesus in a cave,[9] and the virginity of Mary even during *(in partu)* and after *(post partum)* Jesus' birth. Awareness of these traditions generally comes through church doctrine or preaching or the renderings of artists and poets rather than reading of the Protevangelium itself, so that the story itself is little known. Because of the relative unfamiliarity of the Protevangelium, our study of it will begin with an introduction to the Gospel, including some historical considerations generally omitted from the preceding investigations of the canonical Gospels.[10]

The Protevangelium of James opens with the story of the miraculous conception of Mary by the previously childless Joachim and Anna (1:1–5:1). Anna vows to present the child as a gift to the Lord's service. Faithful to her vow, Anna sets the newborn Mary apart by caring for her in a separate bedroom through which nothing impure is allowed to pass. At the age of three, Mary is taken to the Jerusalem temple to live, where she remains until she is twelve years old (5:2–8:1). With the onset of Mary's puberty the priests agree that she can no longer live in the temple, and an angelic messenger instructs that a husband should be found for her among the widowers of Israel. Joseph, who is chosen by a heavenly sign, reluctantly agrees to marry her and takes her to his home (8:2–10:2).

Four years later, Mary receives the angelic annunciation of her pregnancy (11:1–12:3). Discovering the pregnancy, Joseph decides to divorce her, but an angel instructs him otherwise (13:1–14:2). A further crisis develops when the temple priests learn of Mary's pregnancy and subject both Mary and Joseph to the test of bitter waters depicted in Numbers 5:11–31, a test that only confirms the innocence of both parties (15:1–16:2). Joseph and Mary travel to Bethlehem, but they are interrupted en route by Mary's labor. They take shelter in a cave, and there Mary gives birth. The midwife who assists her leaves the cave and proclaims the miracle of Mary's virginity to a passing Salome. Salome scoffs at the news and insists on testing Mary's condition for herself; for this skepticism her hand "falls away, . . . consumed by fire." In response to the instructions of an angel, Salome touches the infant Jesus and instantly receives healing (17:1–20:3). The remainder of the story, which may not be part of the original Protevangelium, concerns the flight to Egypt and the martyrdom of Zacharias at the hands of Herod (21:1–25:1).[11]

The earliest extant manuscript of the Protevangelium opens with the words *genesis Marias apokalypsis Iakōb*, "Birth of Mary, Revelation of James." Given its content, "Birth of Mary" or "Genesis of Mary" would be an appropriate title. Early studies of the text, however, gave it the title "Protevangelium" or "Proto-Gospel," reflecting the fact that the story takes place prior to the narrations of Matthew and Luke. The absorption of this narrative with the figure of Mary, almost to the exclusion of Jesus himself, has prompted recent scholars to question the appropriateness of that title, but the traditional designation is customary and prevents confusion.[12]

Ascertaining anything about the author of the Protevangelium, the time in which it was composed, the community for which it was written, and the purpose that occasioned its composition is exceedingly difficult. We have only such information as can be teased from the text itself. Some of that information is unreliable, and other features of the text can support multiple, even conflicting, conclusions.

At the end of the Protevangelium the writer asserts: "Now I, James . . . wrote this history, when a tumult arose in Jerusalem on the death of Herod" (25:1). The Protevangelium therefore claims James, the brother of Jesus, as its author (although in this gospel James would necessarily be one of Joseph's sons by a prior marriage and thus a step-brother, 9:2). Reference to a disturbance following the death of Herod, presumably Herod the Great, would mean that James composed this story while Jesus was still an infant, indicating that its contents may be regarded as utterly reliable. It is highly improbable, however, that either portion of this statement is accurate.

In fact, scholars generally agree that the Protevangelium was written sometime in the second century. Of the roughly 140 extant Greek manuscripts (manuscripts also exist in Syriac, Georgian, Latin, Armenian, Arabic, Coptic, Ethiopic, and Slavonic), the earliest is Papyrus Bodmer 5, which dates from the fourth, or perhaps even the third, century. The early date of Papyrus Bodmer 5 means that the Protevangelium must have been written by the third century. The fact that Clement and Origen, writing at the end of the second and beginning of the third centuries, display knowledge of the Protevangelium leads to the conclusion that it must have been written by the end of the second century.[13] The astonishingly free method of employing the canonical Gospels suggests that it was written after their composition but before they acquired the status of canon. From these various grounds emerges the consensus that this text comes from the mid- to late second century.[14]

Although his or her name remains unknown, the text itself reveals something of the author's interests. Most revealing is the author's use of the Gospels and the Septuagint. Even the brief summary included above demonstrates that many scenes in the Protevangelium simply retell those in the infancy narratives of Matthew and Luke (although the changes are also dramatic). Not only does the author employ scenes from the Gospels, but he frequently does so with the very wording of the Gospel writers.

The Protevangelium also draws on the Septuagint, using both motifs found in the canonical infancy narratives and others as well. This point is significant, for it means that the author does not simply employ the Septuagint where the canonical Gospels do but reflects independent knowledge of it. Such independence can be seen especially in the Protevangelium's use of stories from the book of Numbers. In order to determine which widower should be married to Mary, an angel instructs the high priest to take the staff of each man and wait for a sign (8:3). Similarly, God instructs Moses to have each of the ancestral houses present a staff and wait for a sign from God indicating which house should serve as Israel's priests (Numbers 17). When Joseph hesitates to be married to Mary, the priest warns him to recall the fate of Dathan, Abiram, and Korah, whose rebellion against the leadership of Moses and Aaron led to their deaths (9:2; Numbers 16). And upon learning of Mary's pregnancy, the high priest subjects both Mary and Joseph to the test of bitter waters instituted in Numbers.

This extensive use of the Old Testament might prompt the suspicion that the author is a Jewish Christian, but much in the Protevangelium is difficult to reconcile with that supposition. To cite but a few dramatic examples, the notion that the young Mary was permitted to live inside the Jerusalem temple could scarcely be credited by anyone who had the slightest acquaintance with temple traditions. Or again, Numbers 5 explicitly states that the test of bitter waters pertains to women who are charged with adultery and never anticipates subjecting men to this same test.[15] The author badly confuses Palestinian geography, so that Joseph and Mary live in Jerusalem but are referred to as residents of Bethlehem (17:1). Taken together, these features of the story probably suggest that the author of the Prot-evangelium was a Gentile Christian who had given considerable attention to the Septuagint as a means of emphasizing the continuity between Mary and Jewish traditions.

Although nothing in the text of the Protevangelium allows us to identify the Christian community for which it was written, several motifs suggest possible concerns of author and church. These concerns can be distinguished as biographical, mariological, and apologetic.[16] Clearly, for the author of the Protevangelium the life of Mary is, in and of itself, an important topic and worthy of discussion. The names of her parents, their disappointment at not having given birth earlier, their care for her as a child, the details of her life in the temple—all these features arise from interest in stories about Mary. The Protevangelium also betrays certain mariological concerns (that is, interests in explicating the theological role of Mary as distinct from biographical concerns), especially regarding the exact nature of Mary's virginity. The desire to explain that Joseph already had children (thus Jesus' brothers are not his biological brothers) and the graphic depiction of Mary's virginity *in partu* go beyond simple biographical detail and in the direction of later mariological discussion. The same may be said for the author's preoccupation with the purity of Mary (about which see below, p. 109–10).

Probably the Protevangelium reflects some of the second-century church's need to defend itself against certain charges from the outside as well as to respond to internal Christian disputes. Claims that Jesus was actu-ally the son of a Roman soldier or that Mary was a poor and outcast woman would find ample response in the Protevangelium's portrayal of her family as wealthy and her virginity as guarded by no less than the temple hierarchy! On the other hand, the midwife's presence at Jesus' birth counters docetic arguments that Jesus was not really a man but only appeared to be human. Discussions such as these occupied Christian thinkers in the second and third centuries and may well have played a role in the formation of the Protevangelium, but it is extremely important to stress the provisional and tentative character of any reconstruction. The Protevangelium provides little material from which to identify the author's own purposes.

Scholars generally agree that the Protevangelium preserves little, per-haps no, historical information about Mary other than what we might glean from the New Testament itself. Such bits of historical information as it might contain present us with the same problem we encounter in canonical accounts: the historical data have been so intertwined with legendary accre-tions that the two can no longer be separated from one another. Probably some of the details contained in the Protevangelium come from oral traditions, legends that invariably grow up around any significant individual. Some details may have come to the author in written form. Others may be the result of the author's own reflection on the Septuagint and the Gospels.[17]

Although the Protevangelium has received more scholarly attention than have many other apocryphal writings, that attention has largely focused on the dating of the text, the manuscript tradition, the possibility that the text contains historical information not available in the New Testament, and the influence of the Protevangelium on later Christian traditions regarding Mary. Our interest lies elsewhere, and, in keeping with earlier chapters, we shall attend to the Protevangelium's characterization of Mary.

THE VIRGIN OF THE LORD

After the virtual silence of the canonical Gospels concerning Mary, the preoccupation with Mary in the Protevangelium comes as a surprise. Here the emphasis shifts from the birth and future greatness of Jesus to the person of Mary herself. Even including chapters 21–24, which may well not have been a part of the original Protevangelium, more than half of this gospel directly concerns itself with the birth, youth, and pregnancy of Mary. The scene depicting Jesus' birth is not an exception to this observation, for there also the narrator focuses on Mary and her astonishing virginity even after having delivered a baby. As a result of these features of the story, one scholar characterizes the Protevangelium as "a (pretty elaborate) mariology in the form of a novel."[18]

The question of how the Protevangelium of James characterizes Mary raises a difficult problem in terminology. Although the author often refers to Mary as the "virgin of the Lord" or the "virgin from the temple of the Lord" (see 9:1, 13:1, 15:2, 16:1; see also 10:1, 19:3), the term *virginity* does not adequately describe her characterization here. Virginity might refer simply to youthfulness or the fact of physical virginity and does not do justice to other elements in the story, such as her years spent in the sanctuary established by Anna or the life apart within the realm of the Jerusalem temple.[19] *Chastity* is even more problematic, because it connotes voluntary sexual abstinence, but Mary makes no conscious choice to renounce sexual relations (except perhaps as she maintains her virginity during Joseph's prolonged absence).

The story itself abounds with the language of purity, as we shall see, but the term *purity* alone can be misleading because of its associations with either moral behavior or the conventions of ritual purity. The Protevangelium betrays little interest in the morality of Mary, if by that we mean her general behavior in relation to other human beings and in conformity with the divine will. The obvious—and significant—exception comes in response to the charges stemming from her pregnancy. Ritual purity refers to those aspects of (in this case) Jewish religious life that govern participation in temple practice. The assumptions of ritual purity do enter the story when Mary reaches adolescence and can no longer live in the temple because a menstruating woman is ritually impure (see Lev 15:19–30). Nevertheless, the purity of Mary in this story vastly exceeds the requirements of ritual purity (e.g., her life in sanctuary before being taken to the temple, her continuing virginity following marriage).

To avoid the limiting or misleading connotations of each of these terms, I have adopted the phrase "sacred purity" to refer to the way in which the Protevangelium portrays Mary. I intend by it a shorthand version of Peter Brown's elegant depiction of Mary in the Protevangelium as "a human creature totally enclosed in sacred space."[20] Mary's purity is established by Anna's care, preserved by the temple priests, guarded by her marriage to Joseph, confirmed during her pregnancy, and finally maintained even as she gives birth. The unfolding drama of the Protevangelium is the drama of maintaining and defending Mary's sacred purity.

Attention to the centrality of Mary's sacred purity in this gospel will raise a number of questions. Does the author of the Protevangelium understand Mary's purity primarily as a way of glorifying her and her son? Does the attention lavished on this feature of Mary create a standard to which the author thinks other Christians should—or must—aspire? By the end of the second century of the Christian era, many Christians evidenced negative attitudes to human sexuality, a development that makes these questions about the Protevangelium both significant and extremely difficult. We shall return to these matters, but only after a more extensive consideration of the Protevangelium and its treatment of Mary.

The drama of Mary in the Protevangelium may be analyzed according to the following acts:

1. The Conception of Mary (1:1–5:1)
2. The Birth and Infancy of Mary (5:2–8:1)
3. The Crisis of Mary's Adolescence (8:2–10:2)
4. The Crisis of Mary's Pregnancy
   a. The Annunciation (11:1–12:3)
   b. The Disclosure to Joseph (13:1–14:2)
   c. The Disclosure to the Priests (15:1–16:2)
5. The Crisis of Mary's Delivery (17:1–20:3)[21]

The Conception of Mary

One prominent contemporary literary theory contends that narratives can be analyzed in terms of some need that must be overcome.[22] Whether or not that generalization holds true for all narrative, certainly a need dominates the first stage of the Protevangelium: the need of Joachim and Anna for a child. Imitative of biblical stories about barren women who miraculously conceive, the Protevangelium dramatically reinforces the customary story of the barren mother by narrating it through parallel scenes. First the author depicts Joachim's humiliation because of his childlessness (1:1–4), then that of Anna for the same reason (2:1–4). This parallel is followed by another in which an angel announces to Anna the promise of a child (3:1–4:1) and then messengers from Joachim bring word that he also has received an angelic annunciation (4:2–4).

Little in this initial stage of the Protevangelium deals directly with Mary, except to signal that a child born under such circumstances must itself be unusual. Anyone familiar with the story of the birth of Isaac or Samuel or John the Baptist would anticipate the birth of an important figure in Israel's history.

That anticipation comes to explicit expression in the angelic announcement to Anna: "Anna, Anna, the Lord has heard your prayer. You shall conceive and bear, and your offspring (lit., "seed") shall be spoken of in the whole world" (4:1). The angel says nothing about why Mary will be spoken of, presumably her role as the mother of Jesus. It is Mary whose significance dominates the text in such a way that a reader who knew nothing about Jesus would have no way of anticipating his birth or later importance.[23]

Before taking up the next act of the Protevangelium, we need to examine two additional issues that arise in this initial act. The first concerns the wealth of Joachim, which appears even in the opening lines of the story: "Joachim was a very rich (man), and he brought all his gifts for the Lord twofold . . ." (1:1). The wealth of Joachim contradicts the poverty of Mary that is at least implied in the Lukan infancy narrative (see Luke 2:24 and Lev 12:8). Within the context of this particular story, Joachim's wealth serves to explain his generosity and makes the rejection of his offering by Reubel even more difficult (1:2).[24]

The second issue has to do with the possibility that the conception of Mary occurs without sexual intercourse between Joachim and Anna. Some contend that the Protevangelium depicts Mary's conception as non-sexual, appealing specifically to 4:2 and 4:4. In the first of these passages, the angel announces to Joachim that Anna has conceived; in the second, Anna herself declares, "I, who was childless, have conceived." Since Joachim has been away from home for some time, the perfect tense of the verb has been understood to mean that Mary's conception occurs without Joachim's participation.

A technical problem complicates this question, because some manuscripts have the future tense in each passage (that is, Anna will conceive) and some have the perfect tense (Anna has conceived). The perfect tense would mean that Anna has conceived in Joachim's absence. However, the perfect tense can be used to connote present action, which means that the issue ought not be decided on the basis of tense alone. More decisive is the fact that the narrative depicts Anna and Joachim as having endured a period of childlessness and consequent shame before their peers, necessitating the conclusion that they have engaged in marital relations and suggesting that the birth of any child to them would occur in the usual way.

The Birth and Infancy of Mary

The events preceding the conception of Mary provide ample indication that she is to be an exceptional individual, but the Protevangelium's major theme of Mary's sacred purity is sounded initially at her birth. After the birth itself, the narrator comments: "And when the days were fulfilled, Anna purified herself from her childbed and gave suck to the child, and called her name Mary" (5:2). Nothing is said of Anna's feeding Mary prior to this rite of purification, although without such feeding the child would surely have died. The point here, of course, is not a biographical note about *when* Mary first ate but the fact that she was fed by a mother who had undertaken the appropriate purification rites. In other words, even from her mother's breast, Mary lived a life of purity.

That impression gains strength in the very next scene, where Anna swears that Mary's feet will not walk upon the ground until she is taken to live in the temple. Anna then "made a sanctuary in her bedchamber, and did not permit anything common or unclean to pass through it. And she summoned the undefiled daughters of the Hebrews, and they cared for her amusement" (6:1). When Mary does go to the temple to live, we read that she was "nurtured like a dove and received food from the hand of an angel" (8:1). Mary's place of living, her food, and her companions all establish the notion that she is to live a pure and undefiled existence.

Already at the annunciation to Anna, the angel declares that Mary will be "spoken of in the whole world" (4:1). The theme of Mary's greatness is developed further by events surrounding her birth and infancy. When Anna attempts to see whether six-month-old Mary can stand, Mary not only stands but walks. She is not merely an astonishing physical prodigy, however. At her first birthday, Mary receives the blessings of the priests in extravagant form: "O God of our fathers, bless this child and give her a name renowned for ever among all generations" (6:2). At the age of three, when she goes to the temple to live, the priest declares: "The Lord has magnified your name among all generations; because of you the Lord at the end of the days will manifest his redemption to the children of Israel" (7:2). If Mary is not herself declared to be Israel's salvation, she here receives a role that is simply astonishing by comparison with the Gospel accounts. "Because of" Mary, God will reveal the redemption of Israel. What exactly the "because of" (epi) means is unclear, but at the very least it assumes some substantive role for Mary.

A small detail at the conclusion of the act underscores Mary's greatness and demonstrates that she accepts sequestered life in the temple not simply with servile obedience but with sheer delight. Following the priest's declaration, the narrator says that the priest puts the child on the third step of the altar, "and the Lord God put grace upon the child, and she danced for joy with her feet . . ." (7:3). Like the faithful of Israel depicted in Ps 149:3, Mary dances before God. This vivid and enchanting picture of a child dancing in the temple epitomizes Mary's sacred purity.

The Crisis of Mary's Adolescence

Following the scene in which Mary has been successfully taken to live in the temple, the narrator passes over the intervening nine years without comment and takes up again with the crisis precipitated by the onset of Mary's adolescence. The problem is indirectly but unmistakably identified by a council of the priests: "Behold, Mary has become twelve years old in the Temple of the Lord. What then shall we do with her, that she may not pollute the sanctuary of the Lord?" (8:2). Historically, of course, a child would not have been allowed to live in the temple at all. In the implied author's conception of the temple, however, that restriction poses no difficulty. What is impossible is that a menstruating woman might live in the temple; hence some action must be taken not only to protect the temple's purity *but also to protect the purity of Mary*. Mary must leave the temple so that she will not pollute it during menstruation. What happens to Mary outside the temple is equally important, however, as this young woman who was promised to God before birth (see 4:1) and has lived in the temple itself cannot be divorced from the sacred realm she has inhabited.

Divine intervention directs the response to this crisis. An angel appears before the high priest to command that the widowers of Israel be gathered together (8:3), and the miraculous appearance of a dove from Joseph's staff indicates that he is the one to whom Mary should be married (9:1). Mary continues to live under divine protection.

Although the Protevangelium here preserves the biblical tradition that Joseph is Mary's husband, the narrator introduces Joseph in a way that makes it clear that this marriage will not involve sexual intercourse. To begin with, the high priest instructs Joseph: "Joseph, to you has fallen the good fortune to receive the virgin of the Lord; take her under your care" (9:1). By depicting her as "virgin of the Lord" and as one to be under Joseph's care, but not referring to her as becoming Joseph's wife, the priest at least implies that Mary is to remain a virgin.

Joseph protests this responsibility, reminding the priest that he himself already has sons and is old, while Mary is but a girl. Responding to the priest's warning about failure to comply with God's will, Joseph does take Mary "under his care."[25] Immediately, however, he leaves Mary while he goes elsewhere to build houses (9:2). The narrator does not explicitly say that Mary and Joseph have refrained from sexual intercourse, however, which leaves at least the shadow of a question regarding their relationship.

That the crisis of Mary's adolescence has been resolved without compromising her purity becomes clear in the final scene in this act of the Protevangelium. The priests decide that the temple requires a veil, and it must be made by the "pure virgins of the tribe of David" (10:1).[26] Seven virgins are found, but in addition the priest recalls "Mary, that she was of the tribe of David and was pure before God." Not only is Mary included with the other virgins in the preparation of the temple veil, but she also is selected to weave the royal segments of purple and scarlet. This action confirms her continuing purity, indeed her surpassing purity, in addition to signaling her connection with the line of David. By the standards of ritual purity, of course, Mary is impure each month for the days of her menstruation, which is why she cannot remain in the temple. That fact does not seem to have anything to do with her sacred purity in the eyes of the author, however.

The Crisis of Mary's Pregnancy

Through the initial acts of the Protevangelium, Mary's purity is established and protected. The onset of her adolescence is a crisis that must be addressed, but it is an inevitable event that does not necessarily entail a compromise of this purity. With her pregnancy, obviously, another crisis ensues. The Protevangelium addresses that crisis by presenting a series of three scenes, each of which asserts Mary's virginity. Here *virginity* is the best word, for it is precisely Mary's physical virginity that is called into question, although that virginity exists as part of her all-encompassing purity.

First, in a scene retelling the Lukan annunciation, she herself questions whether the annunciation regarding her conception means that she will no longer remain a virgin. Second, in a scene retelling the Matthean annunciation, Joseph questions her virginity. Third, the temple priests discover Mary's pregnancy and must be convinced of her virginity.

a. The Annunciation

The annunciation in the Protevangelium follows its Lukan model rather closely. One question is added, however, that bears significantly on the issue of Mary's virginity. In the place of the question Mary asks in Luke 1:34, the Mary of the Protevangelium asks: "Shall I conceive of the Lord, the living God, [and bear] as every woman bears?" (11:2). The reader already knows that Mary is a virgin, but her pregnancy must logically bring an end to that virginity. Mary herself asks the question here, which might be paraphrased as follows: "Does my virginity come to an end?"

In this scene, the narrator speaks, for the first time in the Protevangelium, of the child who is to be born to Mary. Nevertheless, several minor features of the story come together to focus the reader's attention on Mary at least as much as (if not more than) on her son. First, the annunciation itself takes part in two stages. The angel greets Mary when she is outside drawing water. Returning inside, Mary resumes her work. Again the angel confronts her. This interruption heightens the drama and draws attention to Mary. Second, following the annunciation itself, Mary takes her handiwork for the temple veil and presents it to the priest. Nothing is said here of Mary's pregnancy, but he responds to her work with the words: "Mary, the Lord God has magnified your name, and you shall be blessed among all generations of the earth." Third, as in Luke, Mary travels to see Elizabeth, but here no mention is made of the significance of the baby Elizabeth is carrying, and the exchange between Mary and Elizabeth concerns only Mary's maternity.[27]

With the final words of this act, the narrator explains that Mary is sixteen years old when she becomes pregnant (12:3). Since she is twelve when she leaves the temple to marry Joseph, this note regarding Mary's age reinforces the stark difference between the notion of virginity here and that found in the canonical Gospels. There Mary's virginity refers to the fact that she has not been married. Here, by stunning contrast, Mary has remained a virgin through four years of marriage.

b. The Disclosure to Joseph

If Mary's question at the annunciation is subtle ("Shall I conceive of the Lord, the living God, [and bear] as every woman bears?"), the conclusion Joseph must draw when he returns home to find that Mary is six months pregnant is far from subtle. Knowing that he is not the father of the child Mary carries, he must assume that she has engaged in sexual intercourse with someone else. Significantly, his response makes no reference to what would in most cases be interpreted as adultery; instead, he interprets Mary's pregnancy as a violation of her continued status as a virgin of God. The injured party is God, not Joseph.

Joseph laments his situation: "For I received her as a virgin out of the Temple of the Lord my God and have not protected her" (13:1). When he addresses Mary directly, again he speaks of the violation of her sacred purity: "You who are cared for by God, why have you done this and forgotten the Lord your God? Why have you humiliated your soul, you who were brought up in the Holy of Holies and received food from the hand of an angel?" (13:2). These references to Mary's youth recall the elaborate measures taken to secure her purity and serve to dramatize the present crisis. She responds with "I am pure, and know not a man" (13:3), and she further insists that she does not know how she came to be pregnant. This apparent contradiction to the fact that Mary has been told about her pregnancy (11:1–3) probably serves the dramatic purpose of enhancing Joseph's perplexity and leading him to decide that he must divorce her.

As noted earlier, the scene in which Joseph's crisis is resolved draws heavily on Matthew 1:18–25. The instructions given him regarding the child closely parallel those given Mary in 11:2–3. Following the annunciation to Joseph, he "glorified God" and "he kept watch over her" (14:2), thus continuing to carry out the important assignment given him earlier, that of protecting Mary's purity.

One further element in this scene deserves comment. When Joseph initially considers what he presumes has happened to Mary, he asks: "Has the story [of Adam] been repeated in me? For as . . . the serpent came and found Eve alone and deceived her and defiled her, so also it happened to me" (13:1). Here the Protevangelium offers a different sort of Eve-Mary typology from that which develops in other second-century reflection on Mary (see the discussion at the beginning of this chapter). Rather than portray Mary as the New Eve who remains obedient by contrast with Eve's disobedience, Joseph suggests that Mary may be simply the old Eve and Joseph the old Adam! Of course, the angel's instructions to Joseph implicitly reject that typology and rescue Mary from the taint of Eve, but the use of the Adam and Eve story to interpret Mary's story is significant.[28]

c. The Disclosure to the Priests

Assurance that the conception of Jesus does not mean that Mary's purity has been violated comes first and most privately to Mary, then to Joseph, and—most publicly and dramatically—to the priests and all the people. When reports reach the high priest that Mary is pregnant, the charge is that Joseph has defiled "the virgin, whom he received from the temple of the Lord" (15:2) by "stealing marriage" and not disclosing the marriage to Israel. Mary and Joseph are then brought before the high priest, who first accuses Mary of violating the sacred purity of her upbringing. In terms that recall Joseph's earlier accusation against Mary, the high priest accuses her of forgetting her years in the temple, referring specifically to her life in the Holy of Holies, the angels who fed her, her dance before God. When the charges are repeated, the priest further accuses Joseph of consummating the marriage in order that the child thus born to him might be blessed (15:2), as if Mary's very purity could be conveyed to the child. In the face of the denials of both Mary and Joseph, the high priest subjects both of them to the test of bitter waters, a trial that means certain death if they are lying (16:1–2). In Numbers 5, as noted earlier, this test pertains only to women who are accused of adultery, but here it is used for both husband and wife and tests for violation of Mary's virginity within marriage. The ultimate vindication comes when both emerge unharmed from the test and are declared sinless by the high priest: "all the people marvelled" (16:2).

Throughout the crisis to Mary's virginity posed by her pregnancy, the Protevangelium asserts, in ever more public and explicit ways, that she is innocent, and that no fault may be found with her or with Joseph. For the first time, the Protevangelium refers to the child to be born and his role in salvation (11:3; 14:2), but the focus nevertheless remains on Mary. She continues to be a virgin, here interpreted as a sign of the maintenance of the sacred purity that has encapsulated her since birth.

The Crisis of Mary's Delivery

The final act of the Protevangelium, at least as regards Mary, depicts the birth of Jesus.[29] That event, referred to with one phrase in Matthew and scarcely more than that in Luke, here receives considerable attention. Three particular features of this scene convey something of the Protevangelium's understanding of Mary.

First, as Mary and Joseph travel, he notices that she seems sad and then that she is laughing. In response to his natural curiosity, Mary explains: "Joseph, I see with my eyes two peoples, one weeping and lamenting and one rejoicing and exulting" (17:2). This apparent foreshadowing of the division that will be caused by her son recalls the oracle of Simeon in Luke's Gospel (2:29–35) with its warning about Jesus being "destined for the falling and the rising of many in Israel" (2:34). By placing this prophetic word on the lips of Mary, however, the author of the Protevangelium imputes to her the role Luke assigns to Simeon. Given the brief and highly elusive quality of her comment, of course, it is important not to exaggerate its importance. In a gospel that spares only a few words for the baby who is to be born, however, this saying does loom large.

Second, several features of the birth itself convey the presence of the divine in this event. As the midwife approaches the cave where Mary is in labor, a cloud overshadows the cave (19:2), just as clouds often are associated with the presence of the divine (see, e.g., Exod 16:10, 19:9; 1 Kgs 8:10–11; Ps 18:11; Luke 9:34–35). Following the midwife's exclamation, the cloud is displaced by a light greater than human eyes can bear, again a sign of the divine presence (see, e.g., Ps 4:6; Isa 2:5; Acts 9:3, 26:13). When Jesus appears, the narrator explains that the child "went and took the breast of its mother Mary" (19:2). Unlike Anna, who must undergo a purification rite before nursing Mary (see 5:2), Mary is already pure.[30] The birth scene closes when Salome's hand, having fallen off when she dared to inspect Mary after Jesus' birth, is healed simply by the touch of the infant Jesus (20:3–4) and an angel warns her not to tell anyone what she has witnessed.

The third feature of the birth scene bears more directly on Mary herself, and that is the Protevangelium's insistence that Mary continues to be a virgin even as Jesus is born. Following the birth, the midwife exclaims to an otherwise unidentified Salome, "I have a new sight to tell you; a virgin has brought forth, a thing which her nature does not allow" (19:3). This statement could simply refer to the fact that Mary was a virgin at the time of her conception. Salome's response will eventuate in a new interpretation of Mary's virginity, however. Salome objects to the midwife: "As the Lord my God lives, unless I put (forward) my finger and test her condition, I will not believe that a virgin has brought forth" (19:3; cf. John 20:25). For her doubt, Salome's hand falls off as she reaches to touch Mary.

The conclusion to be drawn from this graphic story is that Mary's sacred purity prevails through every challenge, even (or especially) during the birth of Jesus. The purity established by her mother's care, protected by the temple priesthood and then by Joseph, has been maintained not only during conception but during birth itself. Salome's doubt eventuates in a dramatic demonstration that Mary continues to be set apart: she may not be touched. Mary remains the pure "virgin of the Lord."

CONCLUSION

The Protevangelium of James presents us with a Mary who stands at the extreme end of a trajectory that begins with the infancy narratives of Matthew and Luke. They include in their treatments of the birth of Jesus the depiction of his mother as a virgin, but neither evangelist dwells on that topic or seems constrained to account for it or explain it. For Matthew, the virginity of Mary fulfills scripture and carries the potential for scandal that has so often plagued Israel's history. For Luke, the virginity of Mary portrays the power of God to accomplish anything, even that which seems impossible.

The author of the Protevangelium, by contrast, labors to explain the virginity of Mary over and again. If it has not quite become an end in itself, that is because Mary's virginity stands within the framework of an entirely sacred life. Her purity and its preservation simply dominate the story.

In some minor respects, the Mary of the Protevangelium even contradicts the Mary of the Gospels. Luke at least suggests that Mary is from a poor family (Luke 2:24), while in the Protevangelium her father is a wealthy man. In the Protevangelium, her marriage to Joseph occurs when she is twelve years old, and Jesus is conceived when she is sixteen, four years later than the marriage rather than prior to it.

The fundamental difference between the Protevangelium and all of the canonical Gospels, of course, concerns the focal point of the story. In the canonicals, the stories concern Jesus so overwhelmingly that everyone else slips well into the background. What we learn of Mary (or any other character) we learn by teasing every small detail that the story will yield. In the Protevangelium, however, the background and foreground are reversed. From the introduction of Joachim and Anna through the birth of Jesus, Mary and her standing occupy the author's attention. Only with the annunciation to Mary and later to Joseph is the birth of Jesus anticipated. Even when Jesus is born, little is said about his greatness. A reader who knew only the Protevangelium might reasonably conclude that Mary is the holy figure and that Jesus' holiness derives from hers.

The Role of Mary

The prominence given Mary in the Protevangelium arises from her role as the embodiment of sacred purity. The author depicts her separation from the normal realm of life most directly, even graphically, in the drama that surrounds her pregnancy and Jesus' birth. But Mary's sacred purity begins even before her own birth, when Anna sets her apart as one who belongs to God (4:1). Her early years within the temple both protect her from the impurity of the outside world and envelop her within the sacred sphere. That connection continues when she leaves the temple under Joseph's protection, as the frequent references to her temple years and the ongoing involvement of the priests attest. The temple theme in the Protevangelium is far more than a mere recollection of Luke, for it creates a narrative world in which Mary is a part of the sacred realm where the temple also exists.

Mary and Narrative Development

The primary narrative development in the Protevangelium concerns Mary's sacred purity. Established early in the story, her purity is challenged (or at least perceptions of her purity are challenged) by the onset of menstruation, by her pregnancy, and by the birth of Jesus. Each new challenge proves more formidable than the last, and each is answered by more dramatic and miraculous measures than the last.

Mary's purity so dominates this story that she herself is almost a function of that purity rather than the purity being a characteristic of Mary. Perhaps that assertion overstates the case, but certainly little that we think of as "personality" can be ascribed to Mary here. In the synoptic Gospels, Mary receives so little attention that one could scarcely expect to be able to describe her personality or characteristics. In the Protevangelium, she is the center of attention but, nevertheless, her thoughts and responses remain quite hidden from view.

In part, the hiddenness of Mary's personality could be ascribed to the hand of an androcentric tradition that cares little or nothing for the perceptions and desires of women. Such a generalization does not seem to work especially well in this gospel, however, which opens with the touching and extensive depiction of Anna's grief. What does seem clear is that the issue of Mary's purity is of such concern to the author of the Protevangelium that little else matters.

Mary and the "Order" of the Protevangelium

Precisely because of the author's concern for Mary's sacred purity, the question of the "order" of the Protevangelium becomes complicated. What is the nature of Mary's purity and, more important, how is it to be understood by the reader? Does the implied author hope that readers will view Mary as a model and therefore see sexual renunciation as normative for Christians? Or does the implied author expect readers to see in Mary a great exception to the norm, an exception through which salvation enters the world? In other words, what is the function of the purity of Mary?

Certainly Christians who advocated sexual abstinence appealed to the Protevangelium as evidence for their position, but that use of the text does not allow us to conclude that the text itself understands Mary as a model for all Christians in this regard.[31] In fact, the Protevangelium portrays Mary as a great exception.

First, as noted earlier, Mary's purity here is not simply sexual abstinence. She is pure by virtue of where she has lived, who her companions have been, and what she has eaten. She remains pure after her marriage. Mary seems to have less in common with later Christian celibates than with the Vestal Virgins, the Roman priestesses charged with tending the perpetual fire in the temple of Vesta. The Vestals were regarded as holy, but scarcely as a model for all women to emulate.[32]

More important, the Protevangelium does not denigrate the normal means of procreation as do some later Christian writings advocating chastity. The laments of Joachim and Anna over their childlessness are reported positively and their prayers to God are answered. Following the parallel annunciation scenes, the narrator reports that Anna saw Joachim returning home "and ran immediately and hung on his neck" (4:4). The scene concludes that "Joachim rested the first day in his house," which some commentators regard as a delicate way of indicating that the two had sexual relations.[33]

Another way of considering the function of purity in the Protevangelium is to compare it with other Christian texts of this period that clearly do advocate sexual abstinence. The *Acts of Paul,* for example, was composed late in the second century. In that apocryphal writing there can be no doubt that chastity is regarded as normative. Paul himself voices a restatement of the beatitudes that includes:

> Blessed are they who have kept the flesh pure, for they shall become a temple of God.
> Blessed are the continent, for to them will God speak.
> Blessed are they who have renounced this world, for they shall be well pleasing unto God.
> Blessed are they who have wives as if they had them not, for they shall be heirs to God (*Acts of Paul,* 5).[34]

In the story that follows, Paul's preaching persuades a young woman named Thecla to renounce her fiancé and follow Paul's teaching of chastity. The Protevangelium makes no such movement to establish Mary as a pattern for others. Indeed, the movement in the Protevangelium seems to be toward enclosing Mary in sacred purity, and that movement sets her apart from others rather than identifying her as a model to emulate.

In fact, the Protevangelium demonstrates little interest in ethical exhortation of any kind. It concerns itself with the exaltation of Mary as a sacred figure, set apart for God. Some element of apologetic may well be at work here, as Christians respond to the accusations of outsiders about Mary's sexual misconduct or to other Christians who denied the reality of Jesus' humanity. Perhaps the author would have been sympathetic with those who advocated sexual abstinence for Christians, but that sympathy does not come to expression in this text. The Protevangelium focuses, instead, on the sacred purity of Mary and her appropriateness for achieving the redemption of "the children of Israel" (7:2).

NOTES

1. E. R. Dodds, *Pagan and Christian in an Age of Anxiety* (London: Cambridge University, 1965) 3.
2. Especially helpful surveys are Walter J. Burghardt, S.J., "Mary in Western Patristic Thought," in *Mariology*, ed. Juniper B. Carol (2 vols.; Milwaukee: Bruce, 1955, 1957) 1:109–155; "Mary in Eastern Patristic Thought," in *Mariology*, 2:88–153; Hilda Graef, *Mary: A History of Doctrine and Devotion* (2 vols.; London: Sheed and Ward, 1963, 1965) 1:32–100; and Raymond E. Brown, Karl P. Donfried, Joseph A. Fitzmyer, and John Reumann, eds., *Mary in the New Testament* (Philadelphia: Fortress, 1978) 241–82.
3. In this section, wherever possible, quotations from and references to writings of church fathers are from the readily available collection *The Ante-Nicene Fathers,* eds. Alexander Roberts and James Donaldson (10 vols.; Grand Rapids: Eerdmans, 1951–1953), indicated by the abbreviation *ANF* followed by the volume and page number. Full bibliographical information is given for any writings that do not appear in that collection.
4. Burghardt, "Mary in Western Patristic Thought," 132–33.
5. That Jewish interpreters were correct is now conceded by most biblical scholars and is evidenced in the translations of the REB, NJB, NEB, TEV, NRSV.
6. Tertullian likewise argues that Jesus must have been born of a virgin, since otherwise the birth is a normal event and "a daily occurrence—the pregnancy and parturition of a young female, namely—cannot possibly seem anything of *a sign*" (*An Answer to the Jews* 9; *ANF* 3:161).
7. Since this text may indicate that Clement knows the Protevangelium, it by no means contains independent evidence of the early date of this tradition.
8. This generalization is more true of Protestants and perhaps of Roman Catholics than of Christians from Orthodox traditions. The Protevangelium was widely accepted in the Eastern church but condemned in the West by Jerome, by Pope Innocent I, and by the Gelasian Decree. The traditions contained in the Protevangelium, nevertheless, made an impact in the West as well.

9. Justin also says that Jesus was born in a cave (*Dialogue with Trypho* 78; *ANF* 1:237). Justin's comment may reflect his knowledge of the Protevangelium, but it may also be that the author of the Protevangelium knows Justin's comment.

10. See the appendix for the full text of the Protevangelium. Unless otherwise indicated, all quotations from the Protevangelium are from this translation.

11. Presumably as a result of the great interest of earlier generations in the persons and themes of the Protevangelium, it has survived in a large variety of forms that differ significantly from one another.

12. Admittedly, "Protevangelium of James" is an awkward way of referring to this narrative, in that half of the title is Latin and half English. Since it is so referred to in the standard English translation of the New Testament Apocrypha, however, that seems the clearest usage here as well.

13. Clement, *Stromata* 7:16 (*ANF* 2:551); Origen, *Against Celsus* 1:28, 32 (*ANF* 4:408, 410); *In Matthaeum* X, 17 (*PG* 13, 877–78). It is sometimes suggested that even Justin, writing in the mid-second century, reflects awareness of the Protevangelium, but that is much less certain (see above, note 9).

14. For additional discussion of this question and other issues concerning the composition of the Protevangelium, see Oscar Cullmann, "Infancy Gospels," in *New Testament Apocrypha,* vol. 1: *Gospels and Related Writings,* ed. Wilhelm Schneemelcher (rev. ed; Louisville: Westminster, 1991) 421–25; Helmut Koester, *Ancient Christian Gospels: Their History and Development* (Philadelphia: Trinity Press International, 1990) 308–311; Ron Cameron, ed., *The Other Gospels* (Philadelphia: Westminster, 1982) 107–109.

15. Note, however, that the Mishnah, a Jewish legal code written within a century after the Protevangelium, does make a brief and vague reference to the adulterous male who may be destroyed by the test of bitter waters along with the woman (Sotah 5:1 in *The Mishnah,* trans. Herbert Danby [Oxford: Oxford University Press, 1933] 298).

16. H. R. Smid similarly distinguishes biographical, dogmatic, and apologetic concerns. He emphasizes the author's apologetic needs more than I find substantiated in the text (*Protevangelium Jacobi: A Commentary* [Apocrypha Novi Testamenti; Assen: van Gorcum, 1965] 15–20).

17. Willem S. Vorster makes a similar suggestion, namely, that the Protevangelium is a "retelling" of the birth of Jesus, this time from the perspective of Mary ("The Annunciation of the Birth of Jesus in the Protevangelium of James," in *A South African Perspective on the New Testament,* ed. J. H. Petzer and P. J. Hartin [Leiden: Brill, 1986] 33–53; "The Protevangelium of James and Intertextuality," *Text and Testimony,* ed. T. Baarda et al. [Kampen: J. H. Kok, 1988] 262–75).

18. Smid, *Protevangelium,* 19. P. A. van Stempvoort agrees that the Protevangelium is "especially centred on Mary" ("The Protevangelium Jacobi, the Sources of its Theme and Style and their Bearing on its Date," *Studia Evangelica III,* ed. F. L. Cross [Berlin: Akademie Verlag, 1964] 425.)

19. In classical Greece, the term is far more complex, as emerges in Giulia Sissa's fascinating study, *Greek Virginity,* trans. Arthur Goldhammer (Cambridge: Harvard University Press, 1990).

20. Peter Brown, *The Body and Society: Men, Women, and Sexual Renunciation in Early Christianity* (New York: Columbia University Press, 1988) 273.

21. This schematization omits the final section concerning the flight to Egypt and the martyrdom of Zacharias, because those chapters (21–25) scarcely even mention Mary and may not be part of the original form of the Protevangelium.

22. See A. Greimas and J. Cortés, *Semiotics and Language: An Analytical Dictionary* (Bloomington: Indiana University Press, 1982).

23. That is not to suggest that many readers came to the Protevangelium unaware of the identity of either Jesus or Mary. I make the point simply to underscore the way in which interest in Mary dominates this text.

24. Another suggestion often made is that Joachim's wealth provides a response to the anti-Christian slander that Mary was only a poor girl.

25. Much later in the story, Joseph explains to the midwife that Mary is "betrothed" to him (19:1). It is possible that what happens in this earlier passage is that Mary and Joseph become engaged and remain engaged for four years, especially since the text does not explicitly say that they are married. Since she goes to live in his home, however, the implication seems to be that they are married, and that the reference to Mary as "betrothed" in 19:1 reflects assimilation to Luke 2:5. Because the charge lodged against both Mary and Joseph during her pregnancy has to do with violating her purity rather than with adultery, the ambiguity is not terribly important for understanding the story. At the very least, Mary lives under Joseph's protection because of their engagement.

26. The Mishnah discusses the making of two temple veils each year, involving the handwork of eighty-two young girls (Šeqalim 8.5, in *The Mishnah*, 161).

27. C. Clifton Black suggests that the narrator has no need to draw attention to the importance of Elizabeth's child, for the Protevangelium is reassigning to Mary John's task of preparing the way of the Lord (personal letter, July 30, 1993).

28. Georg Kretschmar takes the Eve-Mary contrast to be the primary theme of the Protevangelium, with Mary as the first among the redeemed, in whom the purity of Paradise is restored (" 'Natus ex Maria Virgine': Zur Konzeption und Theologie des Protevangelium Jacobi," in *Anfänge der Christologie: Festschrift für Ferdinand Hahn zum 65 Geburtstag,* ed. C. Breytenbach and H. Paulsen [Göttingen: Vandenhoeck und Ruprecht, 1991] 417–28.)

29. As noted earlier, there is considerable doubt that the scenes concerning the wise men and the martyrdom of Zacharias were part of the original Protevangelium, although it is extremely difficult to ascertain the earliest form of a work for which the manuscript tradition is so diverse. Whatever the earliest form, the role of Mary virtually ends with the birth of Jesus, and the final chapters (21–25) seem quite disconnected from the remainder of the gospel.

30. I owe this observation to the astute reading of C. Clifton Black (personal letter, July 30, 1993).

31. See Peter Brown, *The Body and Society,* for a careful exploration of the several interpretations attached to sexual renunciation in the various forms of Christianity of the second and third centuries.

32. Mary Beard, "The Sexual Status of Vestal Virgins," *JRS* 70 (1980) 12–27. Beard argues that the Vestals were regarded as sacred precisely because they

were anomalous in that they played roles associated both with virgins and with matrons.

33. The difficulty with that interpretation of the comment is that a similar comment appears in 15:1 concerning Joseph; there the narrator certainly does not intend to suggest marital relations.

34. Wilhelm Schneemelcher and Rodolphe Kasser, trans. and eds., "The Acts of Paul," in *New Testament Apocrypha,* vol. 2: *Writings Related to the Apostles,* ed. Wilhelm Schneemelcher (rev. ed.; Louisville: Westminster, 1992) 239.

CHAPTER 6

Glimpses of Mary

Each of the early Christian narratives we have examined permits us a mere glimpse of Mary, the mother of Jesus. She appears in the occasional scene, she utters perhaps a few sentences, and she disappears from sight. Even in the Protevangelium, where Mary occupies center stage during most of the drama, the author is so intently focused on Mary's sacred purity that little else is visible.

Slender and elusive as these glimpses are, they are nevertheless significant. Within all four narratives, Mary serves an important, if often minor, role in the overall development of the story. In Matthew's Gospel, for example, she speaks not a single word, but Matthew introduces through her the powerful thread of the threat to Jesus. In John, her presence at both the wedding in Cana and at the cross reinforces the prologue's claim that, in Jesus, the Word did indeed become flesh.

The glimpses of Mary that we catch in these narratives are also distinctive from one another. How can one reconcile the silent and endangered Mary of Matthew's Gospel with the woman who sets the stage for a miracle in the Gospel of John? Can the rarified Mary of the Protevangelium be the same as the one who ponders and questions in Luke's Gospel? On the other hand, I shall suggest below that each of these glimpses, even with their significant differences, participates in the larger theme of the scandal of the gospel. Before taking up that common thread, I shall briefly review the results of our study.

THE PLURALITY OF THE GLIMPSES

We began with the Gospel of Matthew, where Mary speaks not so much as a single word and is never addressed. She follows in the tradition of the other women in the genealogy, women who were perceived to threaten the Davidic line and who were threatened in return. Because he can only understand her pregnancy as a compromise of his righteousness, Joseph contemplates a divorce that would have grave consequences both for Mary and for her yet-unborn child. Herod sees in the infant Jesus a threat to his own power and therefore acts in a way that threatens both Jesus and his mother. Mary is confined to the role of mother, but in that role introduces an important dynamic in the Matthean Gospel.

In Luke-Acts, Mary plays a more extensive and complex set of roles (disciple, prophet, and mother) than in Matthew. Here she enters the story as a young unmarried woman selected by God to become the mother of Jesus. She consents to this responsibility with the words of a disciple, "Let it be to me according to your word." The story has only begun, however. With the triumphant lines of the Magnificat, Mary takes on the role of a prophet, anticipating leading themes in Luke's Gospel. During the events surrounding Jesus' birth, Luke draws attention to her reflection, anguish, and misunderstanding and anticipates the grief she will suffer at Jesus' death. Luke also insinuates here at the beginning some doubt about whether Mary will continue to be a disciple, a question that is resolved only when she appears in the company surrounding the apostles in Acts 1.

John introduces the mother of Jesus in two brief scenes. First, at the wedding at Cana, she announces to Jesus that the wine has run out, setting the stage for the startling miracle in which Jesus produces a large quantity of wine from water. Second, at the cross, she appears with other women and with the Beloved Disciple, whom Jesus declares to be her son and her to be his mother. These two scenes are connected to the evangelist's statement in 1:14 that the Word became flesh; that is, the mother's presence at Cana underscores the fact that Jesus is a real human being with a mother as well as a human father and brothers (1:45, 2:12). At the cross, when Jesus hands the Beloved Disciple to his mother and her to the Beloved Disciple, he surrenders these earthly relations.

By contrast with the minimal appearance of the mother of Jesus in the Gospel of John, Mary occupies center stage throughout most of the Protevangelium. The author shows an interest in biographical details regarding Mary, particularly in those details that reinforce the sacred purity of Mary. In this narrative Mary herself is born as a result of divine intervention. Even in her infancy she is shielded from any impurity. She grows up living within the temple itself. The onset of puberty prompts a threat to the temple's purity and to Mary's own purity that is resolved when Joseph is selected, again by divine intervention, to be her husband. Her pregnancy prompts a more serious threat to her purity, and three times the story provides assurance that Mary's purity has not been violated. Even the birth of Jesus does not bring an end to Mary's sacred purity.

MARY AND THE SCANDAL OF THE GOSPEL

This brief summary demonstrates that these four narratives present us with different versions of Mary playing different roles in each gospel. Although that plurality of presentations is important and enriching, is it possible to identify any connection among them? As I indicated in chapter 1 of this study, I think it is. All of these glimpses of Mary somehow belong to the theme of the scandal of the gospel, although they do so in very different ways.

With the phrase "the scandal of the gospel," I refer to the multitude of ways in which the Gospels depict Jesus as one whose person and teaching prove offensive to others. Those who become disciples must not take offense, but must be willing to take on the offensiveness of Jesus as their own. As David McCracken has ably put it: "the Gospels are occasions for offense. These occasions are offered in order to bring the reader to belief, but true belief can occur only through the possibility of offense; hence it is more appropriate to call them occasions for offense than occasions for belief, even though the latter is the desirable end."[1]

The glimpses of Mary that we find in the canonical Gospels all participate in this larger scandal of the gospel, although in different ways. This feature of the treatment of Mary appears most visibly in the Gospel of Matthew. Here Mary's name is first introduced in Jesus' genealogy, a genealogy that includes the names of four other women associated with threatening or even scandalous (in the cases of Tamar and Bathsheba) episodes. When Mary herself appears, the reader is told that she is engaged to marry Joseph and is pregnant. Although the narrator carefully explains to the reader that the child is "from the Holy Spirit," that clarification does little to relieve the threat of scandal surrounding her. Only the angel's direct order to Joseph rescues Mary and, by implication, her child from this threat. The scandal of a Jesus who demands a higher standard of righteousness begins early in this narrative, even before his birth.

In Luke-Acts it is not the apparent illegitimacy of Jesus' birth that touches the scandal of the gospel but Mary's struggle to understand Jesus himself. Mary consents readily enough to Gabriel's annunciation, and in the Magnificat she sings forth her exultation even as she interprets its significance. With Jesus' birth, however, she ponders what has taken place. The story of Jesus in the temple at the age of twelve, with which the birth narrative ends, takes Mary's pondering a step further by disclosing a Mary who does not understand Jesus' actions or his words. The question Luke raises in this scene is whether Mary herself will stand among Jesus' disciples or over against him; what will be her response to the scandal of this son who remains in Jerusalem on his own and who insists that he knows what he must be doing? By his skillful treatment of Mary throughout the Gospel, Luke leaves that question open, answering it only when she appears with those gathered in Jerusalem in Acts 1. For Luke, then, Mary participates in the theme of the scandal of the gospel when, like everyone else, she herself is, or at least appears to be, scandalized by Jesus.

The two Johannine scenes in which the mother of Jesus appears put her immediately within reach of scandal. As is clear from the way in which commentators rush to defend both Mary and Jesus, the exchange between the two at the wedding in Cana raises so many questions as to be scandalous in itself. And the scandal of the crucifixion envelops her presence in chapter 19. It is possible to be more specific, however. As the Gospel's way of insisting that Jesus had a human home, the mother of Jesus signals the scandal of Jesus' humanity. Through Mary, the Word becomes flesh and thereby gives offense to the world.

As in many other ways, the treatment of scandal in the Protevangelium of James differs significantly from that of the canonical Gospels. Matthew, Luke, and John accept the fact that scandal is part and parcel of the story of Jesus; indeed, to become a disciple of Jesus is to embrace that scandal.[2] The Protevangelium, however, does not welcome the tension inherent in affirming the scandal of Jesus. Instead, here scandal is graphically depicted and just as graphically dismissed. Not content with the concise assurance of Matthew and Luke that Jesus' conception comes from God, the Protevangelium elaborates on them in several ways. First, the author dissolves any hint of scandal surrounding Mary by depicting her birth and childhood as beyond taint. Second, Joseph is removed from any proximity to Mary (and for four years!), so no one can imagine that Joseph is the father of Mary's child. Third, the test of bitter waters further establishes the innocence of both Mary and Joseph. Fourth, and most dramatically, Salome's thwarted inspection of Mary proves that Mary continues to be a virgin even after Jesus' birth. The Protevangelium of James associates Mary with scandal, but it does so only to show, and with relentless insistence, that the scandal is a vicious lie.

Each of these four narratives reveals a connection between Mary and the scandal of the gospel. Because the connection varies significantly from one narrative to the next, it may appear that the term *scandal* is being used so loosely that the same claim could be made about any character; that is, any Gospel character somehow participates in the scandal surrounding Jesus, and Mary's treatment is in no way distinctive. By no means, however, am I suggesting that only Mary is treated in this way, but neither do I imagine that we could find the same connection in the case of all Gospel characters.

CONCLUDING REFLECTIONS

Having begun this exploration with observations about the multitude of ways in which generations of Christians have portrayed their understandings of Mary in poetry and in painting, it may be appropriate to ask what representations of Mary these narratives suggest for our own time. Three motifs emerge as particularly important.

First and most important is the *vulnerability* of Mary. The word *vulnerability* is somewhat dangerous. I do not wish to portray Mary as a romantic female heroine or as a helpless victim. Nevertheless, *vulnerability* is the right word, for it recalls Matthew's story of her susceptibility to threat from the righteous Joseph and the wretched Herod alike. God's selection of her connects her with other women in the Davidic line who were vulnerable because of their sex but who were preserved by divine intervention. The story of Herod's attempt to destroy her son emphasizes her connection with the child and their common vulnerability.

The Lukan Mary is no less vulnerable. God's selection of her reveals her vulnerability to the One who intervenes in human lives in unexpected ways. Although the vulnerability of Mary takes place in a way restricted to women (since only women bear children), her vulnerability is profoundly shared by many in Luke's story. The seemingly impervious Saul is vulnerable to God's call, a call that radically reverses his actions as persecutor. Peter is vulnerable to God's decision to include Gentiles in a church Peter would have preferred to limit to Jews. Throughout Luke-Acts, the work of the Holy Spirit renders human beings vulnerable. Vulnerability, then, is an unavoidable part of what it means to be a creature of God's making.

Second, Mary is one who *reflects* on events. Although this aspect of Mary appears only in the Gospel of Luke, it warrants careful attention. In the Magnificat she reflects aloud, singing out her praise of God's action in her life and the life of God's people. When Jesus is born, she remembers the events that take place and ponders them. When he acts independently and frighteningly by staying in Jerusalem following Passover, she questions him and again ponders what has taken place. Mary does not wait passively for someone else to explain things to her; she takes an active part by thinking, reflecting, considering matters. Surely if the evangelists explained how John the Baptist or Peter pondered over Jesus, the church would long ago have dubbed these as moments of theological reflection. Because the reflecting subject is a woman, her pondering has been cast in sentimental and trivializing terms. Mary is not writing in the family scrapbook so much as she is initiating Christian reflection.

Third, Mary is among the *witnesses* of Jesus. The Johannine mother of Jesus who stands at the cross does so without a single word. She stands by to watch what takes place, she hears the words of Jesus, and she goes from that place with the Beloved Disciple, given her as a son. By sharp contrast with Peter, who has already denied any association with Jesus, Mary stands by, living out a simple and yet eloquent form of faithfulness. The very quarrels exegetes engage in over the emotional appeal or symbolic value of this scene bespeak the power of Mary's witness.

These features of the Mary of Gospel narratives do not provide us a full picture of Mary, the mother of Jesus. Neither do biblical depictions of Peter or Paul offer us complete characterizations of those individuals. What we do have in these glimpses of Mary are some important aspects of what it means to be a disciple of Christ: living with vulnerability, reflecting with care on the advent of Jesus Christ, and witnessing God's actions in the world. In that sense, Mary remains a model for all Christians.

NOTES

1. David McCracken, *The Scandal of the Gospels: Jesus, Story, and Offense* (New York: Oxford University Press, 1994) 167.
2. That statement is not to deny that the canonical Gospels have apologetic aims among their motives; one of the ways in which they build their defense, however, is to offer a positive interpretation of various aspects of the scandal of Jesus.

The Protevangelium of James

Note: The following translation of the Protevangelium of James is largely based on Papyrus Bodmer 5. Some alternative readings (that is, readings in other manuscripts or editions) that differ from Papyrus Bodmer 5 are enclosed in brackets [ ]. Words or phrases enclosed in parentheses ( ) are clarifications or supplements added by the translator. The translation is that of Oscar Cullmann in *New Testament Apocrypha*, vol. 1: *Gospels and Related Writings,* ed. Wilhelm Schneemelcher (Louisville: Westminster/John Knox, 1991) 426–39.

1.1. In the "Histories of the Twelve Tribes of Israel" Joachim was a very rich (man), and he brought all his gifts for the Lord twofold; for he said in himself: What I bring in excess, shall be for the whole people, and what I bring for forgiveness shall be for the Lord, for a propitiation for me. **2.** Now the great day of the Lord drew near and the children of Israel were bringing their gifts. Then they stood before him, and Reubel [Reuben] also, who said: "It is not fitting for you to offer your gifts first, because you have begotten no offspring in Israel." **3.** Then Joachim became very sad, and went to the record of the twelve tribes of the people, [and said]: "I will search in the record of the twelve tribes of Israel, whether I am the only one who has not begotten offspring in Israel." And he searched and found of all the righteous that they had raised up offspring in Israel. And he remembered the patriarch Abraham that in his last days God gave him a son, Isaac. **4.** And Joachim was very sad, and did not show himself to his wife, but betook himself into the wilderness; there he pitched his tent and fasted forty days and forty nights; and he said to himself: "I shall not go down either for food or for drink until the Lord my God visits me; prayer shall be my food and drink."

2.1. Meanwhile Anna his wife uttered a twofold lamentation and gave voice to a twofold bewailing: "I will bewail my widowhood, and bewail my childlessness."

2. Now the great day of the Lord grew near, and Euthine [Judith] her maidservant said to her: "How long do you humble your soul, for the great day of the Lord is near, and you ought not to mourn. But take this head-band, which the mistress of the work gave me; it is not fitting for me to wear it, because I am your slave and it bears a royal mark."

3. But Anna said: "Away from me! That I will never do. It is the Lord who has greatly humbled me. Who knows whether a deceiver did not give it to you, and you have come to make me share in your sin!" Euthine [Judith] answered: "Why should I curse you because you have not listened to me? The Lord God has shut up your womb, to give you no fruit in Israel."

4. And Anna was very sad; but she put off her mourning-garments, cleansed her head, put on her bridal garments, and about the ninth hour went into her garden to walk there. And she saw a laurel tree and sat down beneath it and [after she had rested] implored the Lord, saying: "O God of our fathers, bless me and hear my prayer, as thou didst bless the womb of Sarah [our mother Sarah] and gavest her a son, Isaac."

3.1. And Anna sighed towards heaven, and saw a nest of sparrows in the laurel tree and immediately she made lamentation within herself:

"Woe to me, who begot me,

What womb brought me forth?

For I was born as a curse [before them all and] before the children of Israel,

And I was reproached, and they mocked me and thrust me out of the Temple of the Lord.

2. Woe, is me, to what am I likened?

I am not likened to the birds of the heaven;

for even the birds of the heaven are fruitful before thee, O Lord.

Woe is me, to what am I likened?

I am not likened to the unreasoning animals;

for even the unreasoning animals are fruitful before thee, O Lord.

Woe is to me, to what am I likened?

I am not likened to the beasts of the earth;

for even the beasts of the earth are fruitful before thee, O Lord.

3. Woe is me, to what am I likened?

I am not likened to these waters;

for even these waters gush forth merrily, and their fish praise thee, O Lord.

Woe is me, to what am I likened?

I am not likened to this earth;

for even this earth brings forth its fruit in its season and praises thee, O Lord."

4.1. And behold an angel of the Lord came to her and said: "Anna, Anna, the Lord has heard your prayer. You shall conceive and bear, and your offspring shall be spoken of in the whole world." And Anna said: "As the Lord my God lives, if I bear a child, whether male or female, I will bring it as a gift to the Lord my God, and it shall serve him all the days of its life."

2. And behold there came two messengers, who said to her: "Behold, Joachim your husband is coming with his flocks; for an angel of the Lord came down to him and said to him: 'Joachim, Joachim, the Lord God has heard your prayer. Go down; behold, your wife Anna has conceived [shall conceive].' " **3.** And immediately Joachim went down and called his herdsmen and said: "Bring me ten lambs without blemish and without spot; they shall belong to the Lord my God. And bring me twelve [tender] calves, and the twelve calves shall be for the priests and elders, and a hundred kids, and the hundred kids shall be for the whole people." **4.** And behold Joachim came with his flocks, and Anna stood at the gate and saw Joachim coming and ran immediately and hung on his neck, saying: "Now I know that the Lord God has richly blessed me [thee]; for behold the widow is no longer a widow, and I, who was childless, have conceived [shall conceive]."

And Joachim rested the first day in his house.

5.1. But the next day he offered his gifts, saying in himself: "If the Lord God is gracious to me the frontlet of the priest will make it clear to me. And Joachim offered his gifts, and observed the priest's frontlet when he went up to the altar of the Lord; and he saw no sin in himself. And Joachim said: "Now I know the Lord God is gracious to me and has forgiven all my sins." And he went down from the Temple of the Lord justified, and went to his house.

2. And her six months [her months] were fulfilled, as (the angel) had said: in the seventh [ninth] month Anna brought forth. And she said to the midwife: "What have I brought forth?" And the midwife said: "A female." And Anna said: "My soul is magnified this day." And she laid it down. And when the days were fulfilled, Anna purified herself from her childbed and gave suck to the child, and called her name Mary.

6.1. Day by day the child waxed strong; when she was six months old her mother stood her on the ground to try if she could stand. And she walked seven steps and came to her mother's bosom. And she took her up, saying: "As the Lord my God lives, you shall walk no more upon this ground until I take you into the Temple of the Lord." And she made a sanctuary in her bedchamber, and did not permit anything common or unclean to pass through it. And she summoned the undefiled daughters of the Hebrews, and they cared for the amusement.

2. On the child's first birthday Joachim made a great feast, and invited the chief priests and the priests and the scribes and the elders and the whole people of Israel. And Joachim brought the child to the priests, and they blessed her, saying: "O God of our fathers, bless this child and give her a name renowned for ever among all generations." And all the people said: "So be it, [so be it] Amen." And they brought her to the chief priests, and they blessed her, saying: "O God of the heavenly heights, look upon this child and bless her with a supreme and unsurpassable blessing." And her mother carried her into the sanctuary of her bedchamber and gave her suck. And Anna sang this song to the Lord God:

> "I will sing a [holy] song to the Lord my God,
>   for he has visited me and taken away from me
>   the reproach of my enemies.
> And the Lord gave me the fruit of righteous-
>   ness, unique and manifold before him.
> Who will proclaim to the sons of Reubel [Reu-
>   ben] that Anna gives suck?
> [Hearken, hearken, you twelve tribes of Israel:
>   Anna gives suck]."

And she laid the child down to rest in the bedchamber with its sanctuary, and went out and served them. When the feast was ended they went down rejoicing and glorified the God of Israel.

7.1. The months passed, and the child grew. When she was two years old, Joachim said to Anna: "Let us bring her up to the Temple of the Lord, that we may fulfil the promise which we made, lest the Lord send (some evil) upon us and our gift become unacceptable." And Anna replied: "Let us wait until the third year, that the child may not long after her father and mother." And Joachim said: "Very well."

2. And when the child was three years old, Joachim said: "Let us call the undefiled daughters of the Hebrews, and let each one take a lamp, and let these be burning, in order that the child may not turn back and her heart be enticed away from the Temple of the Lord." And he did so until they went up to the Temple of the Lord. And the priest took her and kissed her and blessed her, saying: "The Lord has magnified your name among all generations; because of you the Lord at the end of the days will manifest his redemption to the children of Israel."

3. And he placed her on the third step of the altar, and the Lord God put grace upon the child, and she danced for joy with her feet, and the whole house of Israel loved her.

8.1. And her parents went down wondering, praising and glorifying the almighty God because the child did not turn back [to them]. And Mary was in the Temple nurtured like a dove and received food from the hand of an angel.

2. When she was twelve years old, there took place a council of the priests, saying: "Behold, Mary has become twelve years old in the Temple of the Lord. What then shall we do with her, that she may not pollute the sanctuary of the Lord [our God]?" And they [the priests] said to the high priest [to him]: "You stand at the altar of the Lord; enter (the sanctuary) and pray concerning her, and what the Lord shall reveal to you will do."

3. And the high priest took the vestment with the twelve bells and went into the Holy of Holies and prayed concerning her. And behold, an angel of the Lord (suddenly) stood before him and said to him: "Zacharias, Zacharias, go out and assemble the widowers of the people, [who shall each bring a rod], and to whomever the Lord shall give a (miraculous) sign, his wife she shall be." And the heralds went forth and spread out through all the surrounding country of Judaea; the trumpet of the Lord sounded, and all ran to it.

9.1. And Joseph threw down his axe and went out to meet them. And when they gathered together, they took the rods and went to the high priest. The priest took the rods from them and entered the Temple and prayed. When he had finished the prayer he took the rods, and went out (again) and gave them to them: but there was no sign on them. Joseph received the last rod, and behold, a dove came out of the rod and flew on to Joseph's head. And the priest said to Joseph: "Joseph, to you has fallen the good fortune to receive the virgin of the Lord; take her under your care."

2. (But) Joseph answered him: "I (already) have sons and am old, but she is a girl. I fear lest I should become a laughing-stock to the children of Israel." And the priest said to Joseph: "Fear the Lord thy God, and remember all that God did to Dathan, Abiram and Korah, how the earth was rent open and they were all swallowed up because of their rebellion. And now fear, Joseph, lest this happen (also) in your house." And Joseph was afraid, and took her under his care. And Joseph said to her: "Mary, I have received you from the Temple of the Lord, and now I leave you in my house and go away to build [my] buildings; (afterwards) I will come (again) to you; the Lord will watch over you."

10.1. Now there was a council of the priests, who resolved: "Let us make a veil for the Temple of the Lord." And the priest said: "Call to me the pure virgins of the tribe of David." And the officers departed and searched, and they found seven (such) virgins. And the priest remembered the child Mary, that she was of the tribe of David and was pure before God. And the officers went and fetched her.

2. Then they brought them into the Temple of the Lord, and the priest said: "Cast me lots, who shall weave the gold, the amiant, the linen, the silk, the hyacinth-blue, the scarlet and the pure purple." And to Mary fell the lot of the "pure purple" and "scarlet." And she took them and went away to her house. At that time Zacharias became dumb, and Samuel took his place until Zacharias was able to speak (again). But Mary took the scarlet and spun it.

11.1. And she took the pitcher and went forth to draw water, and behold, a voice said: "Hail, thou that art highly favoured, the Lord is with thee, blessed art thou among women." And she looked around on the right and on the left to see whence this voice came. And trembling she went to her house and put down the pitcher and took the purple and sat down on her seat and drew out (the thread).

2. And behold an angel of the Lord (suddenly) stood before her and said: "Do not fear, Mary; for you have found grace before the Lord of all things and shall conceive of his Word." When she heard this she doubted in herself and said: "Shall I conceive of the Lord, the living God, [and bear] as every woman bears?"

3. And the angel of the Lord came and said to her: "Not so, Mary; for a power of the Lord shall overshadow you; wherefore also that holy thing which is born of you shall be called the Son of the Highest. And you shall call his name Jesus; for he shall save his people from their sins." And Mary said: "Behold, (I am) the handmaid of the Lord before him: be it to me according to your word."

12.1. And she made (ready) the purple and the scarlet and brought (them) to the priest. And the priest took (them), and blessed (Mary) and said: "Mary, the Lord God has magnified your name, and you shall be blessed among all generations of the earth."

2. And Mary rejoiced, and went to Elizabeth her kinswoman, and knocked on the door. When Elizabeth heard it, she put down the scarlet, and ran to the door and opened it, [and when she saw Mary], she blessed her and said: "Whence is this to me, that the mother of my Lord should come to me? For behold, that which is in me leaped and blessed thee." But Mary forgot the mysteries which the [arch]angel Gabriel had told her, and raised a sigh towards heaven and said: "Who am I, [Lord], that all the women [generations] of the earth count me blessed?"

3. And she remained three months with Elizabeth. Day by day her womb grew, and Mary was afraid and went into her house and hid herself from

the children of Israel. And Mary was sixteen years old when all these mysterious things happened [to her].

13.1. Now when she was in her sixth month, behold, Joseph came from his
building and entered his house and found her with child. And he smote his
face, threw himself down on sackcloth, and wept bitterly, saying: "With
what countenance shall I look towards the Lord my God? What prayer shall
I offer for her [for this maiden]? For I received her as a virgin out of the
Temple of the Lord my God and have not protected her. Who has deceived
me? Who has done this evil in my house and defiled her (the virgin)? Has
the story [of Adam] been repeated in me? for as Adam was (absent) in the
hour of his prayer and the serpent came and found Eve alone and deceived
her and defiled her, so also it happened to me."

2. And Joseph stood up from the sackcloth and called her [Mary] and
said to her: "You who are cared for by God, why have you done this and
forgotten the Lord your God? Why have you humiliated your soul, you who
were brought up in the Holy of Holies and received food from the hand of
an angel?"

3. But she wept bitterly, saying: "I am pure, and know not a man." And
Joseph said to her: "Whence then is this in your womb?" And she said: "As
the Lord my God lives, I do not know whence it has come to me."

14.1. And Joseph feared greatly and parted from her, pondering what he
should do with her. And Joseph said: "If I conceal her sin, I shall be found
opposing the law of the Lord. If I expose her to the children of Israel, I fear
lest that which is in her may have sprung from the angels and I should be
found delivering up innocent blood to the judgment of death. What then
shall I do with her? I will put her away secretly." And the night came
upon him.

2. And behold, an angel of the Lord appeared to him in a dream, saying:
"Do not fear because of this child. For that which is in her is of the Holy
Spirit. She shall bear [to you] a son, and you shall call his name Jesus; for
he shall save his people from their sins. And Joseph arose from sleep and
glorified the God of Israel who had bestowed his [this] grace upon him, and
he kept watch over her [the maiden].

15.1. And Annas the scribe came to him and said to him: "Joseph, why did
you not appear in our assembly?" And Joseph said to him: "I was weary
from the journey, and I rested the first day." And Annas turned and saw
that Mary was with child.

2. And he went hastily to the priest and said to him: "Joseph, for whom
you are a witness, has grievously transgressed." And the high priest said: "In

what way?" And he said: "The virgin whom he received from the Temple of the Lord, he has defiled, and has stolen marriage with her, and has not disclosed it to the children of Israel." And the high priest said to him: "Joseph has done this?" And [Annas] said to him: "Send officers, and you will find the virgin with child." And the officers went and found her as he had said, and brought her to the Temple. And she stood before the court. And the priest said to her: "Mary, why have you done this? Why have you humiliated your soul and forgotten the Lord your God, you who were brought up in the Holy of Holies, and received food from the hand of angels and heard their hymns of praise and danced before them? Why have you done this?" But she wept bitterly, saying: "As the Lord my God lives, I am pure before him and I know not a man." And the high priest said: "Joseph, why have you done this?" And Joseph said: "As the Lord my God lives [and Christ lives and the witness of his truth], I am pure concerning her." And the high priest said: "Do not give false witness, but speak the truth. You have stolen marriage with her [consummated your marriage in secret], and have not disclosed it to the children of Israel, and have not bowed your head under the mighty hand in order that your seed might be blessed." And Joseph was silent.

16.1 And the high priest said: "Give back the virgin whom you received from the Temple of the Lord." And Joseph wept bitterly. And the high priest said: "I will give you the water of the conviction of the Lord to drink and it will make manifest your sins before your eyes."

2. And the high priest took (it) and gave (it) to Joseph to drink and sent him into the wilderness [into the hill-country]; and he came (back) whole. And he made Mary also drink, and sent her into the wilderness [into the hill-country]; and she (also) returned whole. And all the people marvelled, because (the water) had not revealed any sin in them. And the high priest said: "If the Lord God has not made manifest your sins, neither do I condemn you." And he released them. And Joseph took Mary and departed to his house, rejoicing and glorifying the God of Israel.

17.1. Now there went out a decree from the king Augustus that all (inhabitants) of Bethlehem in Judaea should be enrolled. And Joseph said: "I shall enroll my sons, but what shall I do with this child? How shall I enroll her? As my wife? I am ashamed to do that. Or as my daughter? But all the children of Israel know that she is not my daughter. The day of the Lord itself will do as [t]he [Lord] wills."

2. And he saddled his ass [his she-ass] and sat her on it; his son led it, and Samuel [Joseph] followed. And they drew near to the third mile(stone). And Joseph turned round and saw her sad, and said within himself: "Perhaps that which is within her is paining her." And again Joseph turned round and saw her laughing. And he said to her: "Mary, why is it that I see your face at one time laughing and at another sad?" And she said to him: "Joseph, I see with my eyes two peoples, one weeping and lamenting and one rejoicing and exulting."

3. And they came half the way, and Mary said to him: "Joseph, take me down from the ass [from the she-ass], for the child within me presses me, to come forth." And he took her down there and said to her: "Where shall I take you and hide your shame? For the place is desert."

18.1. And he found a cave there and brought her into it, and left her in the care of his sons, and went out to seek a Hebrew midwife in the region of Bethlehem.

2. [Now I, Joseph, was walking about, and (yet) I did not walk. And I looked up to the vault of heaven, and saw it standing still, and I looked up to the air, and saw the air in amazement, and the birds of heaven remain motionless. And I looked at the earth, and saw a dish placed there and workmen lying round it, with their hands in the dish. But those who chewed did not chew, and those who lifted up anything lifted up nothing, and those who put something to their mouth put nothing (to their mouth), but all had their faces turned upwards. And behold, sheep were being driven and (yet) they did not come forward, but stood still; and the shepherd raised his hand to strike them [with his staff], but his hand remained up. And I looked at the flow of the river, and saw the mouths of the kids over it and they did not drink. And then all at once everything went on its course (again)].

19.1. And he found one who was just coming down from the hill-country, and he took her with him, and said to the midwife: "Mary is betrothed to me; but she conceived of the Holy Spirit after she had been brought up in the Temple of the Lord."

[And behold, a woman came down from the hill-country and said to me: "Man, where are you going?" and I said: "I seek a Hebrew midwife." And she answered me: "Are you from Israel?" And I said to her: "Yes." And she said: "And who is she who brings forth in the cave?" And I said: "My betrothed." And she said to me: "Is she not your wife?" And I said to her: "She is Mary, who was brought up in the Temple of the Lord, and I received her by lot as my wife. And (yet) she is not my wife, but she has conceived of the Holy Spirit." And the

midwife said to him: "Is this true?"
And Joseph said to her: "Come and
see."]

And the midwife went with him. 2. And they went to the place of the cave,
and behold, a dark [bright] cloud overshadowed the cave. And the midwife
said: "My soul is magnified to-day, for my eyes have seen wonderful things;
for salvation is born to Israel." And immediately the cloud disappeared from
the cave, and a great light appeared in the cave, so that our eyes could not
bear it. A short time afterwards that light withdrew until the child appeared,
and it went and took the breast of its mother Mary. And the midwife cried:
"How great is this day for me, that I have seen this new sight." 3. And the
midwife came out of the cave, and Salome met her. And she said to her:
"Salome, Salome, I have a new sight to tell you; a virgin has brought forth,
a thing which her nature does not allow." And Salome said: "As the Lord
my God lives, unless I put (forward) my finger and test her condition, I will
not believe that a virgin has brought forth."

20.1. And Salome went in and made   **1.** And the midwife went in and
her ready   said to Mary: "Make yourself ready,
                                             for there is no small contention con-
                                             cerning you." [And when Mary
                                             heard this, she made herself ready.]
                                             And Salome put forward her finger

to test her condition. And she cried out, saying:

                                             "Woe for my wickedness and my
                                             unbelief; for

"I have tempted the living God; and behold, my hand falls away from me,
consumed by fire!"

2. And she prayed to the Lord.   **2.** And Salome bowed her knees
                                             before the Lord, saying: "O God of
                                             my fathers, remember me; for I am
                                             the seed of Abraham, Isaac and Ja-
                                             cob; do not make me a public
                                             example to the children of Israel, but
                                             restore me to the poor. For thou
                                             knowest, Lord, that in thy name I
                                             perform my duties and from thee I
                                             have received my hire."

3. And behold, an angel of the Lord stood [before Salome] and said to
her: "Salome, God the Lord has heard your prayer. Stretch out your hand to
the child and touch him (take him in your arms), so will healing and joy be
yours." And full of joy Salome came to the child, touched him, [and said:

"I will worship him, for (in him) a great king has been born to Israel."] And Salome was healed at once [as she had requested], and she went out of the cave [justified]. And behold, an angel of the Lord [a voice] cried: "Salome, Salome, tell [not] what marvel you have seen, before the child comes to Jerusalem."

21.1. And behold, Joseph prepared to go forth to Judaea. And there took place a great tumult in Bethlehem of Judaea. For there came wise men saying: "Where is the [new-born] king of the Jews? For we have seen his star in the east and have come to worship him." **2.** When Herod heard this he was troubled and sent officers [to the wise men],

and sent for them and they told him about the star.	[and sent for the high priests and questioned them: "How is it written concerning the Messiah? Where is he born? They said to him: "In Bethlehem of Judaea; for so it is written." And he let them go. And he questioned the wise men and said to them: "What sign did you see concerning the new-born king?" And the wise men said: "We saw how an indescribably greater star shone among these stars and dimmed them, so that they no longer shone; and so we knew that a king was born for Israel. And we have come to worship him. And Herod said: "Go and seek, and when you have found him, tell me, that I also may come to worship him."
3. And behold, they saw stars in the east, and they went before them	**3.** And the wise men went forth. And behold, the star which they had seen in the east, went before them,]

until they came to the cave. And it stood over the head of the child [the cave]. And the wise men saw the young child with Mary his mother, and they took out of their bag gifts, gold, and frankincense and myrrh.

4. And being warned by the angel that they should not go into Judaea, they went to their own country by another way.

22.1. But when Herod perceived that he had been tricked by the wise men he was angry and sent his murderers and commanded them to kill all the children who were two years old and under.

2. When Mary heard that the children were being killed, she was afraid and took the child and wrapped him in swaddling clothes and laid him in an ox-manger.

3. But Elizabeth, when she heard that John was sought for, took him and went up into the hill-country. And she looked around (to see) where she could hide him, and there was no hiding-place. And Elizabeth groaned aloud and said: "O mountain of God, receive me, a mother, with my child." For Elizabeth could not go up (further) for fear. And immediately the mountain was rent asunder and received her. And that mountain made a light to gleam for her; for an angel of the Lord was with them and protected them.

23.1. Now Herod was searching for John, and sent officers to Zacharias at the altar to ask him: "Where have you hidden your son?" And he answered and said to them: "I am a minister of God and attend continually upon his Temple. How should I know where my son is?"

2. And the officers departed and told all this to Herod. Then Herod was angry and said: "Is his son to be king over Israel?" And he sent the officers to him again with the command: "Tell the truth. Where is your son? You know that your blood is under my hand." And the officers departed and told him [all] this.

3. And Zacharias said: "I am a martyr of God. Take my blood! But my spirit the Lord will receive, for you shed innocent blood in the forecourt of the Temple of the Lord." And about the dawning of the day Zacharias was slain. And the children of Israel did not know that he had been slain.

24.1. Rather, at the hour of the salutation the priests were departing, but the blessing of Zacharias did not meet them according to custom. And the priests stood waiting for Zacharias, to greet him with prayer and to glorify God the Most High.

2. But when he delayed to come, they were all afraid. But one of them took courage and went into the sanctuary. And he saw beside the altar of the Lord congealed blood; and a voice said: "Zacharias has been slain, and his blood shall not be wiped away until his avenger comes." And when he heard these words, he was afraid, and went out and told the priests what he had seen [and heard].

3. And they heard and saw what had happened, and the panel-work of the ceiling of the Temple wailed, and they rent their clothes from the top to the bottom. And they did not find his body, but they found his blood turned into stone. And they were afraid, and went out and told [all the people]: "Zacharias has been slain." And all the tribes of the people heard it and mourned him and lamented three days and three nights.

4. And after the three days the priests took counsel whom they should appoint in his [Zacharias'] stead. And the lot fell upon Symeon. Now it was he to whom it had been revealed by the Holy Spirit that he should not see death until he had seen the Christ in the flesh.

25.1. Now I, James who wrote this history, when a tumult arose in Jerusalem on the death of Herod, withdrew into the wilderness until the tumult in Jerusalem ceased. And I will praise the Lord, who gave me the wisdom to write this history. Grace shall be with all those who fear the Lord.

[Nativity of Mary. Apocalypse of James. Peace be to him who wrote and to him who reads!]

Selected Bibliography

Alter, Robert. *The Art of Biblical Narrative*. New York: Basic Books, 1981.

Anderson, Janice Capel. "Mary's Difference: Gender and Patriarchy in the Birth Narratives." *JR* 67 (1987) 183–202.

The Ante-Nicene Fathers. Edited by Alexander Roberts and James Donaldson. 10 vols. Grand Rapids: Eerdmans, 1951–1953.

Aristotle's Poetics. Translated by Leon Golden. Commentary by O. B. Harbison. Tallahassee: University Presses of Florida, 1981.

Ashton, John, ed. *The Interpretation of John*. IRT 9. Philadelphia: Fortress, 1986.

Barth, Karl. *Church Dogmatics*. Vol. 1, Pt. 2: *Doctrine of the Word of God*. Edited by G. W. Bromiley and T. F. Torrance. Edinburgh: T. and T. Clark, 1956.

Bassler, Jouette M. "The Galileans: A Neglected Factor in Johannine Community Research." *CBQ* 43 (1981) 243–57.

Beard, Mary. "The Sexual Status of Vestal Virgins." *JRS* 70 (1980) 12–27.

Beck, David. "The Narrative Function of Anonymity in Fourth Gospel Characterization." *Semeia* 63 (1993) 143–58.

Black, C. Clifton. "Depth of Characterization and Degrees of Faith in Matthew." In *Society of Biblical Literature Seminar Papers 1989*, edited by David J. Lull, 604–23. SBLSPS 28. Atlanta: Scholars, 1989.

Boff, Leonardo. *The Maternal Face of God*. Translated by Robert R. Barr and John W. Diercksmeier. San Francisco: Harper and Row, 1987.

Booth, Wayne. *The Rhetoric of Fiction*. 2nd ed. Chicago: University of Chicago Press, 1983.

Bovon, François. *Das Evangelium nach Lukas: Lk 1,1–9,50*. EKKNT. Zurich: Benziger, 1989.

Boyarin, Daniel. *Carnal Israel: Reading Sex in Talmudic Culture*. Berkeley: University of California Press, 1993.

Brawley, Robert. "Joseph in Matthew's Birth Narrative and the Irony of Good Intentions." *The Cumberland Seminarian* 28 (1990) 69–76.

Brooten, Bernadette J. "Jewish Women's History in the Roman Period: A Task for Christian Theology." In *Christians among Jews and Gentiles*, edited by George W. E. Nickelsburg with George W. MacRae, S.J., 22–30. Philadelphia: Fortress, 1986.

————. *Women Leaders in the Ancient Synagogue*. Brown Judaic Studies 36. Chico, Cal.: Scholars, 1982.

Brown, Peter. *The Body and Society: Men, Women, and Sexual Renunciation in Early Christianity.* New York: Columbia University Press, 1988.

Brown, Raymond E. *The Birth of the Messiah.* Updated edition. New York: Doubleday, 1993.

――――. *The Community of the Beloved Disciple.* New York: Paulist, 1979.

――――. *The Death of the Messiah: From Gethsemane to the Grave.* 2 vols. New York: Doubleday, 1994.

――――. *The Gospel According to John.* AB 29. 2 vols. Garden City: Doubleday, 1966, 1970.

――――, Karl P. Donfried, Joseph A. Fitzmyer, and John Reumann, eds. *Mary in the New Testament.* Philadelphia: Fortress, 1978.

Bulgakov, Sergius. *The Orthodox Church.* Crestwood, N.Y.: St. Vladimir's Seminary Press, 1988.

Bultmann, Rudolf. *The Gospel of John.* Philadelphia: Westminster, 1971.

Burghardt, Walter J., S.J. "Mary in Eastern Patristic Thought." In *Mariology,* edited by Juniper B. Carol, 2:88–153. 2 vols. Milwaukee: Bruce, 1957.

――――. "Mary in Western Patristic Thought." In *Mariology,* edited by Juniper B. Carol, 1:109–55. 2 vols. Milwaukee: Bruce, 1955.

Bussche, Henri van den. *Jean: Commentaire de l'évangel spirituel.* Bible et Vie Chrétienne. Bruges: Desclée de Brouwer, 1967.

Cameron, Ron, ed. *The Other Gospels.* Philadelphia: Westminster, 1982.

Campbell, E. F., Jr. *Ruth.* AB 7. Garden City, N.Y.: Doubleday, 1975.

Cantwell, L. "The Parentage of Jesus [Mt 1:18–21]." *NovT* 24 (1982) 304–315.

Carmichael, C. M. "A Ceremonial Crux: Removing a Man's Sandal as a Female Gesture of Contempt." *JBL* 96 (1977) 332–33.

Carr, Anne. "Mary: Model of Faith." In *Mary, Woman of Nazareth: Biblical and Theological Perspectives,* edited by Doris Donnelly, 7–24. New York: Paulist, 1989.

Charlesworth, J. H., ed. *The Old Testament Pseudepigrapha.* 2 vols. Garden City, N.Y.: Doubleday, 1983, 1985.

Clark, Kenneth. *The Nude: A Study in Ideal Form.* New York: Pantheon, 1956.

Collins, Raymond. "Mary in the Fourth Gospel. A Decade of Johannine Studies." *Louvain Studies* 3 (1970) 99–142.

Conzelmann, Hans. *The Theology of St. Luke.* Translated by Geoffrey Buswell. New York: Harper and Row, 1961.

Craddock, Fred B. *Luke.* Interpretation 42. Louisville: John Knox, 1990.

Cullmann, Oscar. "The Protevangelium of James." In *New Testament Apocrypha.* Vol. 1: *Gospels and Related Writings,* ed. Wilhelm Schneemelcher, 426–39. Rev. ed. Louisville: Westminster/John Knox, 1991.

Culpepper, R. Alan. *Anatomy of the Fourth Gospel: A Study in Literary Design.* Philadelphia: Fortress, 1983.

Darr, John A. *On Character Building: The Reader and the Rhetoric of Characterization in Luke-Acts.* Louisville: Westminster, 1992.

Davies, W. D., and Dale A. Allison. *A Critical and Exegetical Commentary on the Gospel According to Saint Matthew.* Vol. 1: *Introduction and Commentary on Matthew I-VII.* ICC. Edinburgh: T. and T. Clark, 1988.

Davis, Charles Thomas. "The Fulfillment of Creation: A Study of Matthew's Genealogy." *JAAR* 41 (1973) 520–35.

Derrett, J. Duncan M. "Water into Wine." *BZ* 7 (1963) 80–97.

The Documents from the Bar Kokhba Period in the Cave of Letters: Greek Papyri. Edited by Naphtali Lewis. Judean Desert Studies, Vol. 2. Jerusalem: Israel Exploration Society, 1989.

Dodds, E. R. *Pagan and Christian in an Age of Anxiety.* London: Cambridge University Press, 1965.

Fitzmyer, Joseph A. *The Gospel According to Luke.* AB 28. 2 vols. Garden City: N.Y.: Doubleday, 1981, 1985.

————. *Luke the Theologian: Aspects of His Teaching.* New York: Paulist, 1989.

Florovsky, Georges. "The Ever-Virgin Mother of God." In *The Collected Works of Georges Florovsky.* Vol. 3: *Creation and Redemption.* 14 vols. 3: 171–88. Belmont, Mass.: Nordland, 1972–87.

Forster, E. M. *Aspects of the Novel.* New York: Harcourt Brace Jovanovich, 1955.

Freed, Edwin D. "The Women in Matthew's Genealogy." *JSNT* 29 (1987) 3–19.

Garland, David E. *Reading Matthew: A Literary and Theological Commentary on the First Gospel.* New York: Crossroad, 1993.

Gebara, Ivone, and Maria C. Bingemer, *Mary: Mother of God, Mother of the Poor.* Translated by Phillip Berryman. Maryknoll, N.Y.: Orbis, 1989.

Goedt, Michel de. "Un schème de révélation dans le Quatrième Évangile." *NTS* 8 (1962) 142–50.

Graef, Hilda. *Mary: A History of Doctrine and Devotion.* 2 vols. London: Sheed and Ward, 1963, 1965.

Greimas, A., and J. Cortés. *Semiotics and Language: An Analytical Dictionary.* Bloomington: Indiana University Press, 1982.

Gundry, Robert. *Matthew: A Commentary on His Literary and Theological Art.* Grand Rapids: Eerdmans, 1982.

Haenchen, Ernst. *John 1: A Commentary on the Gospel of John Chapters 1–6.* Translated by Robert W. Funk. Hermeneia. Philadelphia: Fortress, 1984.

————. *John 2: A Commentary on the Gospel of John Chapters 7–21.* Translated by Robert W. Funk. Hermeneia. Philadelphia: Fortress, 1984.

Hagner, Donald A. *Matthew.* Vol. 1: *Matthew 1–13.* WBC. Dallas: Word Books, 1993.

Hare, Douglas R. A. *Matthew.* Interpretation 40. Louisville: John Knox, 1993.

Harrington, D. J. *The Gospel of Matthew.* Sacra Pagina 1. Collegeville, Minn.: Liturgical, 1991.

Hengel, Martin. "The Interpretation of the Wine Miracle at Cana: John 2:1–11." In *The Glory of Christ in the New Testament: Studies in Christology in Memory of George Bradford Caird,* edited by L. D. Hurst and N. T. Wright, 83–90. Oxford: Clarendon Press, 1987.

Hochman, Baruch. *Character in Literature.* Ithaca: Cornell University Press, 1985.

Horsley, Richard. *The Liberation of Christmas: The Infancy Narratives in Social Context.* New York: Crossroad, 1989.

Hoskyns, E. C. *The Fourth Gospel.* London: Faber and Faber, 1947.

Johnson, Elizabeth A. "The Marian Tradition and the Reality of Women." *Horizons* 12 (1985) 116–35.

———. "The Symbolic Character of Theological Statements about Mary." *JES* 22 (1985) 312–35.

Johnson, Luke Timothy. *The Gospel of Luke*. Sacra Pagina 3. Collegeville, Minn.: Liturgical, 1991.

Johnson, Marshall. *The Purpose of the Biblical Genealogies with Special Reference to the Setting of the Genealogies of Jesus*. SNTSMS 8. Cambridge: Cambridge University Press, 1969.

Kerrigan, P. Alexander. "Jn. 19, 25–27 in the Light of Johannine Theology and the Old Testament." *Antonianum* 35 (1960) 369–416.

Kingsbury, Jack Dean. *Conflict in Luke: Jesus, Authorities, Disciples*. Minneapolis: Fortress, 1991.

———. *Matthew as Story*. Philadelphia: Fortress, 1986.

———. *Matthew: Structure, Christology, Kingdom*. Philadelphia: Fortress, 1975.

Koester, Helmut. *Ancient Christian Gospels: Their History and Development*. Philadelphia: Trinity Press International, 1990.

Kraemer, Ross Shepard. *Her Share of the Blessings: Women's Religions among Pagans, Jews, and Christians in the Greco-Roman World*. New York: Oxford University Press, 1992.

———. "Jewish Women in the Diaspora World of Late Antiquity." In *Jewish Women in Historical Perspective*, edited by Judith R. Baskin, 43–67. Detroit: Wayne State University Press, 1991.

———, ed. *Maenads, Martyrs, Matrons, Monastics: A Sourcebook on Women's Religions in the Greco-Roman World*. Philadelphia: Fortress, 1988.

Kretschmar, Georg. " 'Natus ex Maria Virgine': Zur Konzeption und Theologie des Protevangelium Jacobi." In *Anfänge der Christologie: Festschrift für Ferdinand Hahn zum 65 Geburtstag*, edited by C. Breytenbach and H. Paulsen, 417–28. Göttingen: Vandenhoeck und Ruprecht, 1991.

Küng, Hans, and Jürgen Moltmann, eds. *Mary in the Churches*. Edinburgh: T. and T. Clark, 1983.

Kurz, William S. "The Beloved Disciple and Implied Readers." *BTB* 19 (1989) 100–107.

Kysar, Robert. *The Fourth Evangelist and His Gospel: An Examination of Contemporary Scholarship*. Minneapolis: Augsburg, 1975.

Laurentin, R. *Structure et théologie de Luc I-II*. Paris: Gabalda, 1957.

Lindars, Barnabas. *The Gospel of John*. NCB. London: Oliphants, 1972.

Luz, Ulrich. *Matthew 1–7: A Commentary*. Minneapolis: Augsburg, 1989.

Macquarrie, John. *Mary for All Christians*. Grand Rapids: Eerdmans, 1990.

Maeckelberghe, Els. *Desperately Seeking Mary: A Feminist Appropriation of a Traditional Religious Symbol*. Kampen, The Netherlands: Kok Pharos, 1991.

Malina, Bruce. "Mother and Son." *BTB* 20 (1990) 54–64.

Marshall, I. Howard. *The Gospel of Luke: A Commentary on the Greek Text*. NIGTC. Grand Rapids: Eerdmans, 1978.

Martyn, J. Louis. *The Gospel of John in Christian History: Essays for Interpreters*. New York: Paulist, 1978.

———. *History and Theology in the Fourth Gospel.* Rev. ed. Nashville: Abingdon, 1979.

McCracken, David. *The Scandal of the Gospels: Jesus, Story, and Offense.* New York: Oxford University Press, 1994.

McHugh, John. *The Mother of Jesus in the New Testament.* Garden City, N.Y.: Doubleday, 1975.

Meeks, Wayne A. "Galilee and Judea in the Fourth Gospel." *JBL* 85 (1966) 159–69.

———. "The Man from Heaven in Johannine Sectarianism." *JBL* 91 (1972) 44–72.

Meier, John P. *A Marginal Jew: Rethinking the Historical Jesus.* Vol. 1: *The Roots of the Problem and the Person.* New York: Doubleday, 1991.

———. *The Vision of Matthew: Christ, Church, and Morality in the First Gospel.* New York: Paulist, 1979.

Merritt, H. Wayne. "The Angel's Announcement: A Structuralist Study." In *Text and Logos: The Humanistic Interpretation of the New Testament,* edited by Theodore W. Jennings, Jr., 97–108. Homage Series. Atlanta: Scholars, 1990.

Meyer, Ben F. " 'But Mary Kept All These Things . . .' (Lk 2, 19.51)." *CBQ* 26 (1964) 31–49.

Meyer, Paul W. "John 2:10." *JBL* 86 (1967) 191–97.

Migne, Jacques-Paul, ed. *Patrologiae Cursus Completus. Series Graeca.* 161 vols. Paris: Lutetiae Parisiorum, 1857–1903.

Minear, Paul S. "The Beloved Disciple in the Gospel of John: Some Clues and Conjectures." *NovT* 19 (1977) 105–23.

———. "Luke's Use of the Birth Stories." In *Studies in Luke-Acts,* edited by Leander E. Keck and J. Louis Martyn, 111–30. Nashville: Abingdon, 1966.

———. *Matthew: The Teacher's Gospel.* New York: Pilgrim Press, 1982.

———. *To Heal and to Reveal: The Prophetic Vocation according to Luke.* New York: Seabury, 1976.

The Mishnah. Translated by Herbert Danby. Oxford: Oxford University Press, 1933.

Moltmann, Jürgen. *The Way of Jesus Christ: Christology in Messianic Dimensions.* Translated by Margaret Kohl. San Francisco: HarperSanFrancisco, 1990.

Neusner, Jacob, William S. Green, and Ernest Frerichs, eds. *Judaisms and Their Messiahs at the Turn of the Christian Era.* Cambridge: Cambridge University Press, 1987.

Neyrey, Jerome H., ed. *The Social World of Luke-Acts: Models for Interpretation.* Peabody, MA: Hendrickson, 1991.

Nissiotis, Nikos. "Mary in Orthodox Theology." In *Mary in the Churches,* edited by Hans Küng and Jürgen Moltmann, 25–39. Edinburgh: T. and T. Clark, 1983.

O'Day, Gail R. *Revelation in the Fourth Gospel.* Philadelphia: Fortress, 1986.

Ouspensky, Leonid. *Theology of the Icon: Volume I.* Translated by Anthony Gythiel. Crestwood, NY: St. Vladimir's Seminary Press, 1992.

Overman, J. Andrew. *Matthew's Gospel and Formative Judaism: The Social World of the Matthean Community.* Minneapolis: Fortress, 1990.

Painter, John. *The Quest for the Messiah: The History, Literature and Theology of the Johannine Community.* 2nd ed. Edinburgh: T. and T. Clark, 1993.

Pamment, Margaret. "The Fourth Gospel's Beloved Disciple." *ExpTim* 94 (1983) 363–67.

Patte, Daniel. *The Gospel according to Matthew: A Structural Commentary on Matthew's Faith.* Philadelphia: Fortress, 1987.

Phelan, James. *Reading People, Reading Plots: Character, Progression and the Interpretation of Narrative.* Chicago: University of Chicago Press, 1989.

Plank, Karl A. "The Human Face of Otherness." In *Faith and History: Essays in Honor of Paul W. Meyer,* edited by John T. Carroll, Charles H. Cosgrove, and E. Elizabeth Johnson, 55–73. Homage Series. Atlanta: Scholars, 1990.

Powell, Mark Allan, ed. *The Bible and Modern Literary Criticism.* Bibliographies and Indexes in Religious Studies 22. New York: Greenwood, 1992.

———. *What Are They Saying About Luke?* New York: Paulist, 1989.

———. *What Is Narrative Criticism?* Minneapolis: Fortress, 1990.

Price, Martin. *Forms of Life: Character and Moral Imagination in the Novel.* New Haven: Yale University Press, 1983.

Rahner, Karl. *Mary: Mother of the Lord.* New York: Herder and Herder, 1963.

Räisänen, Heikki. *Die Mutter Jesu im Neuen Testament.* Helsinki: Suomalainen Tiedeakatemia, 1969.

Rimmon-Kenan, Shlomith. *Narrative Fiction: Contemporary Poetics.* London: Methuen, 1983.

Ruether, Rosemary Radford. *Mary: The Feminine Face of the Church.* Philadelphia: Westminster, 1977.

Schaberg, Jane. *The Illegitimacy of Jesus: A Feminist Theological Interpretation of the Infancy Narratives.* San Francisco: Harper and Row, 1987.

Schnackenburg, Rudolf. *The Gospel According to St. John.* 3 vols. New York: Crossroad, 1982.

Schneemelcher, Wilhelm, and Rodolphe Kasser, trans. and ed. "The Acts of Paul." In *New Testament Apocrypha.* Vol. 2: *Writings Related to the Apostles,* edited by Wilhelm Schneemelcher, 213–70. Rev. ed. Louisville: Westminster/John Knox, 1992.

Schüssler Fiorenza, Elizabeth. "Feminist Theology as a Critical Theology of Liberation." *TS* 36 (1975) 605–26.

Senior, Donald. *What Are They Saying About Matthew?* New York: Paulist, 1983.

Sissa, Giulia. *Greek Virginity.* Translated by Arthur Goldhammer. Cambridge: Harvard University Press, 1990.

Sloyan, Gerard. *John.* Interpretation. Atlanta: John Knox, 1988.

Smid, H. R. *Protevangelium Jacobi: A Commentary.* Apocrypha Novi Testamenti. Assen: van Gorcum, 1965.

Smith, D. Moody. *Johannine Christianity: Essays on Its Setting, Sources, and Theology.* Columbia: University of South Carolina Press, 1984.

———. *John.* Proclamation Commentaries. 2nd ed. Philadelphia: Fortress, 1986.

———. *John Among the Gospels: The Relationship in Twentieth-Century Research.* Minneapolis: Fortress, 1992.

Spong, John Shelby. *Born of a Woman: A Bishop Rethinks the Birth of Jesus.* San Francisco: HarperSanFrancisco, 1992.

Springer, Mary Doyle. *A Rhetoric of Literary Character: Some Women of Henry James.* Chicago: University of Chicago Press, 1978.

Stacpoole, Alberic, OSB. "Mary's Place in *Lumen Gentium,* Vatican II's Constitution on the Church." In *Mary and the Churches,* edited by Alberic Stacpoole, OSB, 85–97. Dublin: Columba Press, 1987.

Staley, Jeffrey Lloyd. *The Print's First Kiss: A Rhetorical Investigation of the Implied Reader in the Fourth Gospel.* SBLDS 82. Atlanta: Scholars, 1988.

Stanton, Graham, ed. *The Interpretation of Matthew.* IRT 3. Philadelphia: Fortress, 1983.

Stempvoort, P. A. van. "The Protevangelium Jacobi, the Sources of its Theme and Style and their Bearing on its Date." *Studia Evangelica III,* edited by F. L. Cross, 410–26. Berlin: Akademie Verlag, 1964.

Stendahl, Krister. "Quis et Unde?" In *Judentum, Urchristentum, Kirche: Festschrift für Joachim Jeremias,* edited by Walther Eltester, 94–105. BZNW 26. Berlin: Alfred Töpelmann, 1960.

Sternberg, Meir. *The Poetics of Biblical Narrative: Ideological Literature and the Drama of Reading.* Bloomington: Indiana University Press, 1985.

Strycker, Emile de. *De Griekse handschriften van het Protevangelie van Jacobus: De protevangelii Iacobi codicibus graecis.* Brussel: Paleis der Academien, 1968.

Talbert, Charles H. "Jesus' Birth in Luke and the Nature of Religious Language." *Heythrop Journal* 35 (1994) 391–400.

———. "Prophecies of Future Greatness: The Contribution of Greco-Roman Biographies to an Understanding of Luke 1:5–4:15." In *The Divine Helmsman: Studies on God's Control of Human Events Presented to Lou Silberman,* edited by J. L. Crenshaw and S. Sandmel, 129–41. New York: KTAV, 1980.

———. *Reading John: A Literary and Theological Commentary on the Fourth Gospel and the Johannine Epistles.* New York: Crossroad, 1992.

Tambasco, Anthony J. *What Are They Saying About Mary?* New York: Paulist, 1984.

Tannehill, Robert C. "The Magnificat as Poem." *JBL* 93 (1974) 263–75.

———. *The Narrative Unity of Luke-Acts: A Literary Interpretation.* Vol. 1: *The Gospel According to Luke.* Philadelphia: Fortress, 1986.

Terrien, Samuel. *The Magnificat: Musicians as Biblical Interpreters.* Mahwah, N.J.: Paulist, 1995.

Testuz, Michel, ed. *Papyrus Bodmer V: Nativité de Marie.* Cologne: Bibliotheca Bodmeriana, 1958.

Thompson, Marianne Meye. *The Humanity of Jesus in the Fourth Gospel.* Philadelphia: Fortress, 1988.

Trible, Phyllis. *God and the Rhetoric of Sexuality.* Philadelphia: Fortress, 1978.

Unnik, W. C. van. "*Dominus vobiscum:* The Background of a Liturgical Formula." In *New Testament Essays: Studies in Memory of Thomas Walter Manson,* edited by A. J. B. Higgins, 270–305. Manchester: Manchester University Press, 1959.

Via, Dan O., Jr. "Narrative World and Ethical Response: The Marvelous and Righteousness in Matthew 1–2." *Semeia* 12 (1978) 123–49.

Vorster, Willem S. "The Annunciation of the Birth of Jesus in the Protevangelium of James." In *A South African Perspective on the New Testament,* edited by J. H. Petzer and P. J. Hartin, 33–53. Leiden: Brill, 1986.

———. "The Protevangelium of James and Intertextuality." In *Text and Testimony,* edited by T. Baarda et al., 262–75. Kampen: J. H. Kok, 1988.

Warner, Marina. *Alone of All Her Sex: The Myth and the Cult of the Virgin Mary.* New York: Vintage, 1976.

White, Hayden. "The Value of Narrativity in the Representation of Reality." In *The Content of the Form: Narrative Discourse and Historical Representation,* 1–25. Baltimore: Johns Hopkins University Press, 1987.

Biblical and Other Ancient Sources

Other Christian Literature

Modern Authors

Alter, Robert, 21–22, 47n7

Baarda, T., 123n17
Barr, Robert R., 25n28
Barth, Karl, 16–17, 26n47
Baskin, Judith R., 24n10
Basore, John W., 77n26
Bassler, Jouette M., 98n11
Beard, Mary, 124n32
Beck, David, 99n17
Berryman, Phillip, 25n29
Bingemer, Maria Clara, 14
Black, C. Clifton, 27n69, 124n27, 124n30
Boff, Leonardo, 13
Booth, Wayne, 75n2
Bovon, François, 77n32
Boyarin, Daniel, 7, 24n16
Brawley, Robert, 48n15
Breytenbach, C., 124n28
Bromiley, G. W., 26n47
Brooten, Bernadette J., 7, 24n6
Brown, Peter, 110, 124n20, 124n31
Brown, Raymond E., 19, 25n19, 30–31, 47n3, 47n6, 48n11, 48n13, 48n14, 48n19, 50, 51, 56, 64, 76n4, 76n5, 76n9, 76n10, 76n12, 76n14, 76n15, 77n21, 77n25, 77n30, 77n35, 85–86, 98n7, 99n16,122n2
Bulgakov, Sergius, 26n43
Bultmann, Rudolf, 99n15
Burghardt, Walter J., 122n2, 122n4

Bussche, Henri van den, 99n25
Buswell, Geoffrey, 76n3

Cameron, Ron, 123n14
Campbell, E. F., Jr., 47n8
Carmichael, C. M., 47n8
Carol, Juniper B., 122n2
Carr, Anne, 14
Carroll, John T., 48n18
Cather, Willa, 2
Charlesworth, J. H., 23n1, 77n24
Clark, Kenneth, 21
Clifton, Lucille, 1, 24n2, 49
Collins, J. J., 77n24
Collins, Raymond, 99n24, 99n25
Colson, F. H., 24n9
Conzelmann, Hans, 50
Cortés, J., 124n22
Cosgrove, Charles H., 48n18
Cross, F. L., 123n18
Cullmann, Oscar, 123n14, 133
Culpepper, Alan, 27n66

Danby, Herbert, 24n7, 123n15
Darr, John A., 28n78
DeLacy, Phillip H., 77n29
Diercksmeier, John W., 25n28
Dodds, E. R., 101, 122n1
Donaldson, James, 122n3
Donfried, Karl P., 25n19, 48n11, 122n2
Donnelly, Doris, 25n35